The
Descendants of

JACOB and MARY
MOOMEY

of Pennsylvania, Maryland, Ohio and Iowa

Dale Douglas Webster

ֆֆᏣᏣ

HERITAGE BOOKS
2006

HERITAGE BOOKS

AN IMPRINT OF HERITAGE BOOKS, INC.

Books, CDs, and more—Worldwide

For our listing of thousands of titles see our website
at
www.HeritageBooks.com

Published 2006 by
HERITAGE BOOKS, INC.
Publishing Division
65 East Main Street
Westminster, Maryland 21157-5026

International Standard Book Number: 978-0-7884-2495-5

Dedication

This genealogy is dedicated to my father, Reginald Dale Webster. He inherited the strength and tall stature that our family lore says came from his Moomey ancestors. Reggie loved his family and was proud of his pioneer heritage.

TABLE OF CONTENTS

TABLE OF FIGURES

Reading This Book

If, while reading the following pages of this book, the reader will keep these few facts in mind, a much clearer understanding of the contents will result. The format or style used in this book is known as the **Modified Register System,** which has been refined by the National Genealogical Society.

Three types of numbers are used: one to uniquely identify the individual, one to indicate the generation into which that person falls, and one to denote his or her birth-order within the nuclear family. The identification numbering system used in this book is called **By Generation.** The starting person is 1; his first child is 2. All the children are listed as generation number two, the grandchildren are listed as generation number three and so on. Each person is assigned an ID number in sequential order by generation.

When an individual is introduced in his/her separate sketch, the name appears in boldface letters with the surnames in all capital letters. The identification number precedes the name. The last given name is followed immediately by a superscript number indicating the number of generations from the starting individual in this book. In parentheses following the name is a list of direct ancestors back to the starting individual. Only the given name is listed, preceded by his/her ID number, and followed by the generation number in superscript.

When the list of children is presented, the plus (+) sign indicates that more about this child will be presented in his/her separate sketch. The ID number is printed, followed by M/F indicating the sex. Next a small roman numeral in front of the name designates birth-order. Next the name is followed by the birth and death dates.

The term "Spouse" may have several different meanings: husband, wife, partner, mate, or significant other. The couple involved may not be legally married. The term "stepchild" may have several different meanings: the child may be a stepchild, adopted child, foster child, or just raised in the home. If there are any other children of the spouse, they will be designated as stepchildren.

The index is arranged alphabetically by surname. Under each surname, the given names are alphabetically arranged. The name is followed by the year of birth and death in square brackets. The number to the right indicates the page where this name appears. The wife appears under her maiden name and under her married names with her maiden name in parentheses.

Acknowledgments

Prominent among the family member researchers was the late Howard E. Webster of Iowa. His efforts with the assistance of his wife, Bernice, started this work and deserve much of the credit.

Charlotte Moomey of Omaha, Nebraska, also contributed her excellent research into her family.

Also, I have special thanks to my Aunt Elaine (Webster) Wilson for much of the valuable family information presented here and to my wife, Kathleen, for editorial assistance and encouragement.

CHAPTER 1

The Descendants of
Jacob and Mary Moomey of
Pennsylvania, Maryland, Ohio, and Iowa

Listing 370 descendants for 7 generations.

GENERATION NO. 1

The background of the German people is very interesting. Rome was never able to conquer the Teutonic German tribes of northern Europe. For most of the last 2,000 years, Germany consisted of about 600 little fiercely independent monarchies, principalities, and duchies. They were brought into the empires of Charlemagne and Frederick the Great of Prussia only briefly. However, when Napoleon defeated the Prussian army in 1806 and occupied Germany until 1815, the desire for unification grew and finally came about in 1871.[1]

Conflict during the 1700s and 1800s between the many German states, Prussia, and France resulted in the destruction of many homes and farms, forced military conscription of sons, and required lodging and feeding of occupying armies. This situation motivated many families to escape this tyranny and immigrate to the United States to

---

[1] Atmore, Anthony et al, *The Last Two Million Years,* The Reader's Digest Association, 1973, London, pages 390 and 391.

1

seek a better life in this wonderful land of opportunity. Our Moomey German ancestors were among these people and will be discussed in this part.

1. **Jacob[1] MOOMEY** was born 1789 in Lancaster County, Pennsylvania.[2] He was the son of John Jacob MOOMEY. Jacob died 24 September 1872 in Moscow, Muscatine County, Iowa, at the age of 83.[3] He married **Mary Magdalene BRUNER** 15 June 1811 in Lancaster, Fairfield County, Ohio.[4] She was born 16 March 1793 in Maryland.[5] She was the daughter of Johan Jacob BRUNER and Christina SATTLER. Mary died 1883 in Keokuk, Iowa, at the age of 89.

They had 9 children:

+ 2.   f   i.   **Christina MOOMEY**, born 24 June 1812, died 13 March 1894.
+ 3.   m   ii.   **John MOOMEY**, born 1813, died after 1860.
+ 4.   f   iii.   **Mary Magdalene MOOMEY**, born 29 July 1816, died 19 March 1902.

---

[2] From ages given in various censuses and affidavits, Jacob's possible birth date ranges from June 2, 1786 to April 15, 1790.

[3] War of 1812 military and pension records at the National Archives (Application 26926, Certificate 18306, Widow's Application 9589, Widow's Certificate 6017, and Bounty Land Warrants 48,933-40-50 and 70,668-120-55).

[4] National Archives War of 1812 Application #26926.

[5] Although it was first believed Mary was born in Pennsylvania, the 1850 Census in Ohio lists her birthplace as Maryland

+ 5. m iv. **Jacob MOOMEY, Junior,** born 1823.
+ 6. f v. **Betsy MOOMEY,** born 1826, died 1 April 1880.
+ 7. m vi. **Peter MOOMEY,** born 9 March 1829, died 22 August 1913.
+ 8. f vii. **Catherine MOOMEY,** born December 1831.
   9. m viii. **Henry MOOMEY,** born 1833 in Seneca County, Ohio, died, and was buried in Osceola, Clark County, Iowa.
  10. m ix. **Christian MOOMEY,** born 1835 in Seneca County, Ohio.

Census takers, who were not always accurate, spelled the Moomey surname from 1820 to 1870 in the following ways: Mummy, Mooney, Moomis, Mumey, Mooney, and Moomey. Entries in the 1820, 1830, and 1840 censuses are only assumed to be them, since family members were not named, but the locations seem to fit.

The Moomey (Moomy or Mummy) family was German speaking and among the many German immigrants to come into Maryland and Pennsylvania in the late 1700s. Jacob and Mary's son Peter spoke no English until about age 11 when he started school, and, even after he was married, his parents often used German rather than English.

Jacob was a farmer. He had an uneventful enlistment in the Ohio Militia in the War of 1812 where he marched up into Quebec but was not involved in any engagements.

3

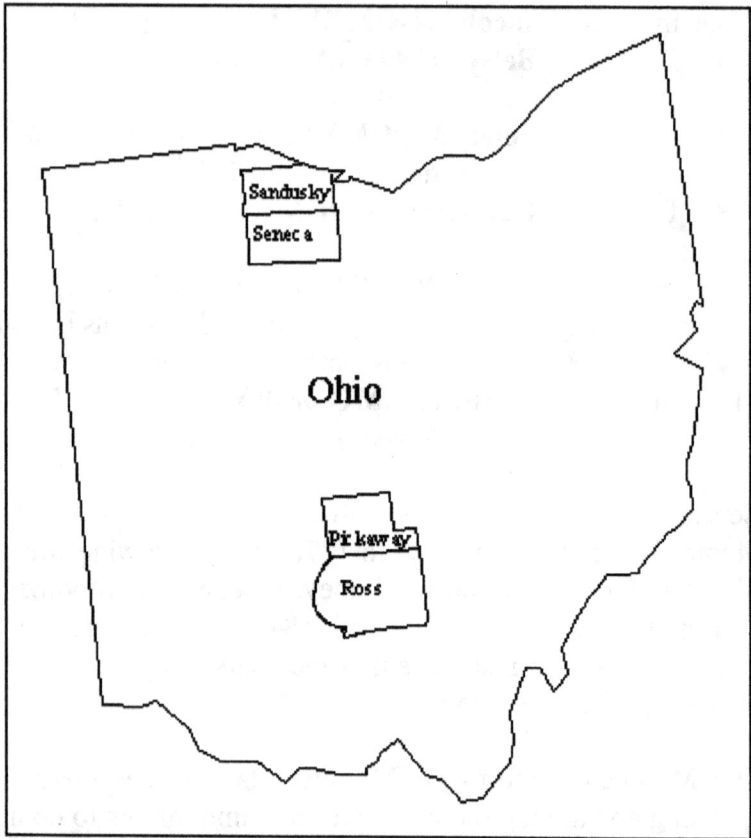

Figure 1 – Map of Ohio showing relevant points.

The 1820 census indicates they were in adjoining Pickaway County, Ohio, in Washington Township which is near Circleville. By 1830, they were in Ballville Township in Sandusky County. In 1840 and 1850, they were living in adjoining Pleasant Township of Seneca County. This 1850 household showed Jacob age 63, Mary 61, Peter 21, Catherine 19, and also Jefferson 5 and Clarissa 3. The last

4

two were probably grandchildren. Adjoining households were those of son John and Elizabeth, son-in-law John Webster and Mary Magdalene, son Jacob and his wife Effa, and a Mary Bruner, age 81, living with a Mary Bruner, 14.

In 1851, Jacob's family and some of his married children moved to Iowa, when he was granted bounty land for his War of 1812 service.[6] According to a Tama County, Iowa history biography of one of Mary's brothers, Christian Bruner (born 1799 in Pennsylvania), this was "before there was even a railroad in the state." Christian Bruner had 19 children of two wives. His biography goes on to say, "Some of the children, of course, married and remained in Ohio, but when the family started for the west in wagons, it made quite a colony in itself. A start was made in the fall of 1851; on the way the Bruners were joined by the Overmires, and the strengthened party spent the following winter in Iowa City, and in the spring of 1852 located in Tama County." John and Mary Moomey Webster had a son born December, 1851, in Iowa City, Johnson County, Iowa.

Jacob settled in Johnson County, receiving 40 acres of bounty land. In 1856, he received an additional grant of 120 acres. During this time, Jacob also operated a fanning mill, which separated grain from chaff.

---

[6] National Archives Bounty Land Warrants: Act of 28 September, 1850, #143821. 48,933_40_50 for 40 acres of Iowa land and Act of 3 March, 1855; 70,668_120_55. for 120 acres of Iowa land.

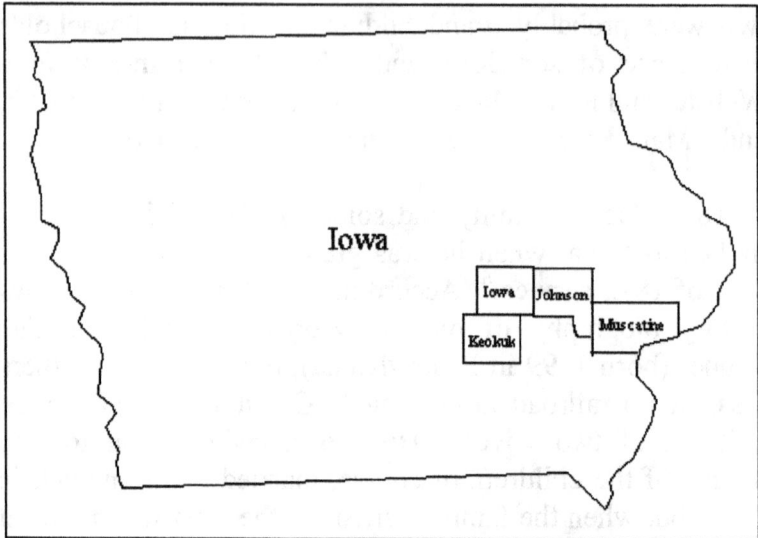

Figure 2 – Map of Iowa showing relevant points.

In 1860, Jacob and Mary Moomey were in Union Township of Johnson County. Peter's family was in the adjoining household. Their post office was Iowa City.

About 1869, Peter's family moved to Muscatine County, where Peter had a butcher business. The 1870 Census shows Jacob and Mary, now about 80 years old, in Peter's household in Wilton Township, Wilton Junction. Jacob died in adjoining Moscow Township on September 24, 1872.

About that time, Peter's family moved to Keokuk County, when the butcher business failed. Peter again took up farming as a tenant. In the 1880 Census, Mary was still living with them; her age was given as 87. It has been told that when she was about 90 or so, she went with Peter's family to visit relatives in Iowa County, about 30 miles away and a very full day's ride. She made the trip seated in a rocking chair in the wagon and was described as robust.

Family legend has it that Jacob's father, John Jacob Moomey, was a Revolutionary War soldier. The most likely candidate I could find in the National Archives was a pension application R16627 (The "R" means Rejected) submitted by a John Mummy who in 1829 was living in Circleville, Pickaway County, Ohio where Jacob and Mary were living during the 1820 Census. He says that he enlisted in the Continental Army and served in the Battle of Brandywine, which we lost. He was captured by the British and imprisoned in Philadelphia. When the British left Philadelphia, he escaped, made his way back to his home in the mountains of western Maryland, got married, and never bothered to find his unit.

Mary Magdalene Bruner's father was also named Jacob. There is confusion by researchers over where Jacob Bruner was born. According to census and family records he was born about 1770. According to legend in the Martin Bruner family, he was born in Strausberg, a village east of Berlin, Germany and came here with his widowed mother about 1791-2. The same legend has it that his father had been affluent and a soap manufacturer in Strausberg. The ship "Fair American" had on board two passengers, Jacob Bronner and Maria Dorothea Bronner, listing her first, as cabin passengers, landing in September, 1791 at Philadelphia. Legend has it that the mother brought her son to America to save him from conscription in the Prussian

Army at the start of the Napoleonic Wars. The family was believed to have been Jewish.

There was also a Jacob Bronner born in 1770 in Lancaster County, Pennsylvania to Casper Brunner and Ursula Shellenberger. There is a town called Strausberg in Lancaster County.

It is possible that Jacob Bruner married three times. The name of his first wife, Christina Sattler, is taken from the baptismal certificate of Christina Bruner Zehrung. It could have been spelled Sattler, Staller, Stadler, etc. Nothing further was found on her. She was definitely dead by October, 1812 when Jacob married Margaret Ebright of Bright in Fairfield, Pickaway County, Ohio. However, according to the Martin Bruner family, Martin had no idea he was not a full brother to the other children until he was an adult. This might lead one to suspect that Christina died between 1803 (birth of Margaret) and 1807 when Martin was born and Jacob had married again. The son, Peter, was most likely by Margaret Ebright as she was in his favor and against the other children in legal documents partitioning land in Seneca County, Ohio.

CHAPTER 2

GENERATION NO. 2

This generation, the children of Jacob and Mary Moomey, saw and participated in the expansion of the United States to new frontiers. They also lived through the horrors of the Civil War. These people were pioneers who settled in the wilderness, fought the Indians, and overcame many obstacles to raise their families.

2. Christina[2] **MOOMEY** (1.Jacob[1]) was born 24 June 1812 in Circleville, Pickaway County, Ohio. She was the daughter of Jacob MOOMEY and Mary Magdalene BRUNER. Christina died 13 March 1894 in Decatur County, Iowa, at the age of 81, and was buried in LeRoy Church Cemetery, Decatur County, Iowa. She married **George WISEMAN**. He was born 1808 in Circleville, Pickaway County, Ohio.

They had 6 children:

11.	m	i.	**Peter WISEMAN.**
12.	m	ii.	**Jacob WISEMAN.**
+ 13.	f	iii.	**Susan Ann WISEMAN**, born 31 March 1851.
14.	m	iv.	**Adam WISEMAN.**
15.	m	v.	**Aaron WISEMAN.**
16.	f	vi.	**Mary WISEMAN.**

Christina and George were living in Moscow Township, Muscatine County, Iowa in October, 1872.

- - - - - - - - - -

3. John² MOOMEY (1.Jacob¹) was born 1813 in Circleville, Pickaway County, Ohio. He was the son of Jacob MOOMEY and Mary Magdalene BRUNER. John died after 1860 in Near Homestead, Amana Colonies, Iowa. He married (1) **Elizabeth** [————?————]. She was born 1817 in Circleville, Pickaway County, Ohio.

They had 6 children:

17. f   i.   **Martha Jane MOOMEY**, born 1837 in Ohio. She married (1) **Henry STRING** 1856. Martha married (2) **C. P. LYON** 1860.

18. m   ii.   **John MOOMEY**, born 1840.

19. f   iii. **Louisa MOOMEY**, born 1842. She married _____ **OSBORNE**.

+ 20. m   iv.   **Henry Washington MOOMEY**, born 1 November 1846, died 20 March 1933.

+ 21. m   v.   **LeRoy MOOMEY**, born 22 March 1851, died 22 July 1953.

22. f   vi.   **Caroline MOOMEY**.

John married (2) **Marie TALBOT**.

No children have yet been identified.

In 1850, John and Elizabeth lived in Pleasant Township, Seneca County, Ohio, next door to his parents. In 1856, John is listed as a widower with four children, John, Louisa, Henry, and LeRoy, in Hartford Township, Iowa County, Iowa. He was a carpenter who helped build some of the first houses at Homestead, Iowa, now a part of the Amana Colonies. His second wife was "the widow Talbot" who had a farm west of Homestead.

- - - - - - - - - - -

4. Mary Magdalene² MOOMEY (1.Jacob¹) was born 29 July 1816 in Circleville, Pickaway County, Ohio. She was the daughter of Jacob MOOMEY and Mary Magdalene BRUNER. Mary died 19 March 1902 in Greene Twp., Iowa County, Iowa, at the age of 85, and was buried in Bethel Cemetery, Washington Twp., Johnson County, Iowa. She married **John H. WEBSTER** 26 May 1836 in Sandusky County, Ohio.⁷ He was born 4 February 1814 in New York.⁸ He was the son of Samuel WEBSTER and Deborah FULLER. John died 15 March 1876 in Green Twp., Iowa County, Iowa, at the age of 62, and was buried in Bethel Cemetery, Johnson County, Iowa.⁹

They had 10 children:

+ 23. m   i.   **Simeon M. WEBSTER**, born 13 March 1837, died 24 December 1865.

+ 24. f   ii.   **Harriet WEBSTER**, born 7 September

---

⁷ Marriage information comes from early records at the Hayes Memorial Library at Fremont, Ohio.

⁸ John Webster was an identical twin. Birth record source is entry in an account book, which his twin brother David probably maintained. The account book also showed the birth dates of his children. The middle initial "H" is seen in an 1840 census of Sandusky County, Ohio.

⁹ John died of Typhoid fever at his home in Iowa County, Iowa on March 15, 1876.

1838, died 20 November 1916.

+ 25.   m   iii.   **William Daniel WEBSTER**, born 16 August 1840, died 6 April 1927.

+ 26.   m   iv.   **M. Lafayette WEBSTER**, born 1 September 1842, died about 1923.

  27.   f   v.   **Malinda WEBSTER**, born 7 April 1845 in Seneca County, Ohio, died 26 November 1862 in Iowa, at the age of 17. Died of typhoid fever at age 17.

  28.   m   vi.   **Jacob WEBSTER**, born 15 February 1847 in Seneca County, Ohio, died in infancy 8 October 1847 in Seneca County, Ohio, and was buried in Decker Cemetery, Sandusky County, Ohio.

+ 29.   f   vii.   **Nancy WEBSTER**, born 21 June 1849, died 29 January 1918.

+ 30.   m   viii.   **Frehling Sylvester WEBSTER**, born 19 December 1851, died 24 January 1929.

  31.   m   ix.   **John Charles WEBSTER**, born 17 March 1856 in Iowa County, Iowa, died 27 May 1925, at the age of 69, and was buried 28 May 1925 in Oakland Cemetery, Iowa City, Johnson County, Iowa. He was never married and was crippled by rheumatic fever as a young man. He lived all his life with his brother

Freling.

32. f   x.   **Emma Josephine WEBSTER**, born 15 June 1859 in Iowa County, Iowa, died in childhood 15 May 1864 in Iowa, at the age of 4. Died of typhoid fever.

In 1850, she and her family lived in Pleasant Township, Seneca County, Ohio, next to her brother John and her parents. John and Mary Webster moved from Ohio to Iowa in 1851. Their last three children were born in Iowa. Heading the party coming from Ohio to Iowa were Jacob Moomey and his wife Mary Magdelene (Bruner) Moomey. Jacob Moomey was a veteran of the War of 1812 and received bounty land in Iowa for that service. This grant of bounty land was the motivation for the move of a large extended family. Besides his son-in-law, John Webster, and daughter, Mary Magdelene, Jacob's daughter, Christina, and her husband, George Wiseman, also came. In addition, Jacob Moomey's sons, John, Jacob, and Peter, and their families came to Iowa in this large family group.

John and Mary Webster purchased a farm for $150 in Green Township, Iowa County, Iowa and lived good lives there. My late Cousin Howard Webster, an avid family history researcher, shared some remembrances of the Webster homestead:

"I lived until I was 18 on the old Webster homestead where Great Grandfather John and Mary Webster settled after moving from Ohio. The farm is still in the family. My

brother, Wayne, owns it today. No one lives on the place, because the old house got into such bad condition, the cost of restoration would have been very great, so we felt we would had to tear it down. We hated to see it go because of all the memories associated with it. Grandfather Frehling and his brother, John, lived with us, so I grew up hearing them tell of their own boyhoods and all the happenings in the family. Frehling and John were around ten years old when the Civil War started. Their brother, Daniel, was in the war and several other cousins. Frehling and John said they were most unhappy that they could not go off to war.

There was a large and beautiful grove of native hardwood trees surrounding the Webster home and much of this grove of trees was still there when I was living there. Great Grandfather was a licensed preacher in the United Brethren Church and as long as he was living he would conduct services for the family and others who cared to come. In the summer, services were in the grove of trees. When his daughter, Harriett, got married, the ceremony was also in the grove.

Great Grandfather also started a brick factory and a drain tile factory as well as a sawmill near his home on the banks of Old Mans Creek, a smallish river or large creek. They first built a log and earth dam on the creek and ran the mill with waterpower but later secured a steam engine. He made the bricks used to build his home and also sawed the lumber for it.

My Grandfather, Frehling, and his brother, John,

lived on in the old home with their mother after the death of John in 1872, and for a while their brother, Lafayette, helped operate the brick factory, but, in later years, Lafayette moved to Long Beach, California, and a Mr. Hiram Frank became a partner in the brick factory. Mr. Frank was a bachelor and lived with the Webster family. About 1909, they sold the factory and all the equipment, and the new owner only operated it for about two years when the steam engine blew up setting fire to the wooden buildings housing the machinery, the drying shed, etc., and all was destroyed by this fire. Today, one can tell where the kiln was because of the numerous brick fragments."

Figure 3 – John Webster's Brick Factory (Circa 1870)

Figure 4 – John and Mary Webster (Circa 1860).

Figure 5 – The children of John and Mary Webster.
Standing from left: Harriet, John Charles, and Nancy.
Seated from left: William Daniel, M. Lafayette, and
Frehling Sylvester.
(Circa 1870)

Family lore has it that Mary was taller than John and that the Webster men owe their tall stature to their Moomey genes.

- - - - - - - - - -

5. Jacob² MOOMEY, Junior (1.Jacob¹) was born 1823 in Ohio. He was the son of Jacob MOOMEY and Mary Magdalene BRUNER. He married **Effa** [————?————]. She was born 1827 in Ohio.

They had 1 child:
33. f i. **Cordelia MOOMEY**, born 1844.

In 1850, Jacob Junior lived next door to his parents in Pleasant Township, Seneca County, Ohio. In August of 1852, he bought a lot in Iowa City, Iowa, near the courthouse. He and Effa deeded it out the next May. In December 1853, Jacob Senior drew up a Letter of Attorney to Jacob Junior to set up a fan mill business in Iowa City but not to incur debts in Jacob Senior's name.

- - - - - - - - - -

6. Betsy² MOOMEY (1.Jacob¹) was born 1826 in Seneca County, Ohio. She was the daughter of Jacob MOOMEY and Mary Magdalene BRUNER. Betsy died 1 April 1880, at the age of 54, and was buried in Bethel Cemetery, Washington Twp., Johnson County, Iowa. She married **Aaron ANDREW**. He was born 31 January 1826. Aaron died 18 August 1901, at the age of 75, and was buried in Bethel Cemetery, Johnson County, Iowa.

They had 3 children:
34. m i. **Newton ANDREW**, born in Sandusky

County, Ohio. He married **Ella YOAKAM.**

35. m   ii.   **Riley ANDREW.** He married **Elsie CROSS.**

36. m   iii.   **Leon ANDREW.** He married _____ **SMITH.**

- - - - - - - - - -

7. Peter² MOOMEY (1.Jacob¹) was born 9 March 1829 in Sandusky County, Ohio. He was the son of Jacob MOOMEY and Mary Magdalene BRUNER. Peter died 22 August 1913 in Mason City, Custer County, Nebraska, at the age of 84, and was buried in Mason City, Custer County, Nebraska. He married **Jane H. HANLON** 5 December 1858 in Johnson County, Iowa. She was born 12 February 1839 in Stubenville, Ohio. She was the daughter of William HANLON. Jane died 19 June 1926 in Hastings, Nebraska, at the age of 87, and was buried in Mason City, Custer County, Nebraska.

They had 6 children:

37. m   i.   **Otis H. MOOMEY,** born 27 July 1859 in Richland, Iowa. He married **Ella M. STRICKLAND** 4 July 1879. Otis died 22 August 1925, at the age of 66.

38. m   ii.   **John E. MOOMEY,** born 1874 in Iowa.

39. m   iii.   **Freeling Sylvester MOOMEY,** born 10 January 1875 in Keokuk County, Iowa. He married **Harriet Roseta ROLOSON** 1894.

Freeling died 16 November 1932, at the age of 57.

40. m iv. **Wesley W. MOOMEY**, born 4 August 1876 in Keota, Keokuk County, Iowa. He married **Minnie P. CASTELOW** 19 February 1899. Wesley died 8 August 1950 in York, Nebraska, at the age of 74.

41. m v. **William R. MOOMEY**, born in Iowa.

42. f vi. **Eletty B. MOOMEY**, born in Iowa.

- - - - - - - - - -

8. Catherine² MOOMEY (1.Jacob¹) was born December 1831 in Ohio. She was the daughter of Jacob MOOMEY and Mary Magdalene BRUNER. Catherine died in Des Moines, Polk County, Iowa, and was buried in Des Moines, Polk County, Iowa. She married **William A. DIXON** 8 January 1853. He was born December 1831 in Illinois.

They had 3 children:

43. m i. **Charles W. DIXON**, born 1860 in Illinois.

+ 44. f ii. **Minerva "Minnie" DIXON**, born 18 March 1865, died 8 March 1937.

45. m iii. **Herbert C. DIXON**, born 1871 in Illinois.

They were not found in the 1860 Census.

The 1870 Census showed them in Tazewell, Little Mackinaw, Iowa. William was listed as a builder and Catherine as a housekeeper.

The 1880 Census shows them in Keota, Keokuk, Iowa. He is a house carpenter and she keeps house. They had the three known children: Charles W. who was 20 and a farm laborer, Minnie who was 15 and Herbert who was 8. Both William and Catherine are buried in Iowa.

CHAPTER 3

GENERATION NO. 3

The grandchildren of Jacob and Mary Moomey lived in the last half of the 1800s and the first part of the 1900s. They helped tame the West and saw the expansion of the United States to the Pacific Ocean. The railroads were built during their lives and revolutionized travel and commerce for them.

13. Susan Ann³ WISEMAN (2.Christina², 1.Jacob¹) was born 31 March 1851. She was the daughter of George WISEMAN and Christina MOOMEY. She married **William Robert WADE** 10 March 1870. He was born 13 November 1846. William died 14 August 1921, at the age of 74.

They had 13 children:

46. f   i.   **Lulu Helen WADE,** born 19 December 1870. She married **Bert Ramsey STENINGER** 5 November 1895. Lulu died 17 July 1943, at the age of 72.

47. f   ii.   **Martha Gay WADE,** born 29 September 1872. She married **William I MILLER** 31 December 1891. Martha died 27 November 1899, at the age of 27.

48. m   iii.   **Albert Otis WADE,** born 29 September 1874. He married **Mary E. CLAYPOOL** 26 April 1900.

49. f   iv.   **Jennie May WADE,** born 29 April 1877.

50. m   v.   **Alexis George WADE,** born 23 May 1880. He married **Edith**

CHAPMAN 21 March 1906.

51. m   vi. **William John WADE,** born 2 June 1882. He married **Bertha TRACY** 30 September 1907.

52. m   vii. **Orastes Arthur WADE,** born 1 October 1884. He married **Lavera MISSENGER.** Orastes died 24 October 1918, at the age of 34.

53. f   viii. **Dora Matilda WADE,** born 11 April 1886, died in infancy 2 September 1887.

54. f   ix. **Armintie Estella WADE,** born 29 March 1888. She married **Herbert DeFRANCE** 29 December 1904.

55. f   x. **Mary Alta WADE,** born 20 January 1891.

56. f   xi. **Hettie WADE,** born 16 August 1893, died in infancy 31 August 1893.

57. f   xii. **Etta WADE,** born 16 August 1893, died in infancy 31 August 1893.

58. f   xiii. **Bessie Fern WADE,** born 9 October 1894. She married **James E. CURL** 27 November 1912.

In October, 1872, they were living in Moscow Township, Muscatine County, Iowa.

- - - - - - - - - - -

20. Henry Washington[3] MOOMEY (3.John[2], 1.Jacob[1]) was born 1 November 1846 in Seneca County, Ohio. He was the son of John MOOMEY and Elizabeth [———?———] . Henry died 20 March 1933 in Iowa Soldiers Hospital, Marshalltown, Iowa, at the age of 86, and was buried in

Maple Hill Cemetery, Osceola, Clarke County, Iowa. He married **Clarinda C. BONHAM** 17 December 1868 in Windham, Johnson County, Iowa. She was born 14 April 1849. Clarinda died 28 October 1927 in Osceola, Clarke County, Iowa, at the age of 78, and was buried in Maple Hill Cemetery, Osceola, Clarke County, Iowa.

They had 3 children:

59. m   i.   **Frank H. MOOMEY**, born 4 December 1868 in Clarke County, Iowa. He married **Carrie SANDERS** 29 October 1891. Carrie died 1911. Frank died 2 July 1946, at the age of 77.

+ 60. m   ii. **Clarence Mitchell MOOMEY**, born 29 March 1873, died 9 April 1950.

61. f   iii. **Maude I. MOOMEY**, born 7 September 1878 in Iowa, died 25 July 1897, at the age of 18, and was buried in Frytown Cemetery, Johnson County, Iowa. In 1880, Henry and Clarinda were living in Knox Township, Clarke County, Iowa.

Henry was a Civil War veteran. He had a full set of teeth and all his hair when he died. He never swore or had an unkind word about anyone.

- - - - - - - - - -

21. LeRoy³ MOOMEY (3.John², 1.Jacob¹) was born 22 March 1851 in Seneca County, Ohio. He was the son of John MOOMEY and Elizabeth [———?———] . LeRoy died 22 July 1953 in Kalona, Washington County, Iowa, at the age of 102, and was buried in Frytown Cemetery, Johnson County, Iowa. He married **Cora FRY** 3 January 1874 in Johnson County, Iowa. She was born 1858 in Johnson County, Iowa. Cora died March 1935, at the age of 77, and was buried in Frytown Cemetery, Johnson County, Iowa.

They had 2 children:

+ 62. m   i.   **Bruce MOOMEY**, born 14 July 1876, died 1951.

63. m   ii.   **Cullen MOOMEY**, born 20 May 1886 in Iowa. He married **Ambert MORGAN**. Cullen died 27 July 1978, at the age of 92.

LeRoy lived on a farm near his first cousin Frehling Webster in Johnson County, Iowa. He lived for a while with Frehling and worked at the Webster brick and tile factory and saw mill. About 1936, he lived with his son Bruce in Iowa City. He was very spry and raised garden produce for sale. Later, he lived with his sister Louisa Lyons at Belle Plaine, near Amana.

- - - - - - - - - - -

23. Simeon M.³ WEBSTER (4.Mary², 1.Jacob¹) was born 13 March 1837 in Sandusky, Erie County, Ohio. He was the son of John H. WEBSTER and Mary Magdalene MOOMEY. Simeon died of typhoid fever 24 December 1865 in Woodbine, Johnson County, Iowa, at the age of 28, and was buried in Bethel Cemetery, Johnson County, Iowa. He married **Eliza Hannah YOAKAM** 10 July 1858 in Woodbine, Johnson County, Iowa. She was born 31 July 1839 in Marion County, Ohio. She was the daughter of

Joseph YOAKAM and Nancy HIGGINS. Eliza died 21 April 1921 in Woodbine, Johnson County, Iowa, at the age of 81, and was buried in Bethel Cemetery, Johnson County, Iowa.

They had 3 children:

64. f i. **Mary E. WEBSTER**, born 6 April 1860. She married **John R. TUPPER**.

65. m ii. **Laurence WEBSTER**, born 1862, died in childhood 15 October 1864, at the age of 2.

66. m iii. **Joseph Norman WEBSTER**, born 12 May 1865. He married **Cora T. SCULL**. Joseph died in 1955 at 90 years old, and was buried in Woodbine, Iowa.

- - - - - - - - - - -

24. Harriet³ WEBSTER (4.Mary², 1.Jacob¹) was born 7 September 1838 in Sandusky County, Ohio. She was the daughter of John H. WEBSTER and Mary Magdalene MOOMEY. Harriet died 20 November 1916, at the age of 78, and was buried in Moulton, Iowa. She married **Virgil FRY**. He was born 1834 in Sandusky County, Ohio.

They had 4 children:

67. m i. **Charles Sylvester FRY**, born August 1859, died 1 November 1913, at the age of 54.

68. m ii. **Frank L. FRY**, born November 1860.

69. f iii. **Kate O. FRY**, born February 1862. She married **A. E. MAIN**.

70. f iv. **Mary Jane FRY**, born September 1864.

She   married   _____
GARRETT.

- - - - - - - - - -

25. William Daniel³ WEBSTER (4.Mary², 1.Jacob¹) was born 16 August 1840 in Seneca County, Ohio.[10] He was the son of John H. WEBSTER and Mary Magdalene MOOMEY. William died 6 April 1927 in Gypsum, Saline County, Kansas, at the age of 86, and was buried in Canton, McPherson County, Kansas. He married (1) **Laura AUGUSTINE** 1860 in Iowa. She was born 1839 in Iowa. Laura died 1873 in Iowa City, Iowa, at the age of 34.

They had 5 children:

71. m   i.   **Charles Eugene WEBSTER**, born 27 April 1861, died 12 September 1882 in Family Farm, Roxbury, Kansas, at the age of 21. Died due to a kick in the head by a horse and is buried on the farm in a field beside the Lindsberg-Roxbury Road.

+ 72. m   ii. **William Wesley WEBSTER**, born 7 March 1863, died 25 October 1933.

+ 73. f   iii. **Almyra May WEBSTER**, born 8 September 1865.

---

[10] William's birth date was obtained from his Civil War pension records at the National Archives. Birth dates of the children were obtained from the 1910 U.S. Census at Kansas, Marion County, Lehigh Township, Sheet 8B.

+ 74. m   iv.   **John Ellsworth WEBSTER**, born 6 April 1869, died 21 March 1941.

75. f   v.   **Florence WEBSTER**, born 8 October 1871.

According to my Aunt Elaine, Florence went on the "stage" and was disowned by her father for it. She was heard of only once more when she wrote her brother John that she would be at the Canton railroad station and would like to see him. Even though John was married at the time and living in a home of his own, he did not dare go against his father's wishes and go see his sister.

William had 1 stepchild:

+ 76. m   vi.   **Clarence B. AUGUSTINE.**

William married (2) **Nancy Jane JESTER** 3 January 1874 in Iowa City, Johnson County, Iowa. She was born 12 May 1853 in Mt. Pleasant, Henry County, Iowa.[11] She was the daughter of John Charles "Jesse" JESTER and Elizabeth Amanda WHITE. Nancy died 20 April 1931 in Canton, McPherson County, Kansas, at the age of 77, and was buried in Canton, McPherson County, Kansas.[12]

They had 14 children:

+ 77. m   vii.   **Marion Jonas WEBSTER**, born 21 December 1874, died

---

[11] Nancy's birth, marriage, and death information were obtained from William Daniel Webster's Civil War pension records from the National Archives.

[12] Kansas death certificate #59 3632.

21 October 1932.

78. f viii. **Electra Ann WEBSTER**, born 1 May 1876 in Iowa, died in childhood 16 September 1878 in Iowa, at the age of 2.

+ 79. f ix. **Mary Etta WEBSTER**, born 16 March 1877.

+ 80. m x. **Virgil Franklin WEBSTER**, born 31 January 1879, died 25 July 1962.

+ 81. m xi. **Howard Lincoln WEBSTER**, born 16 October 1881, died 27 November 1969.

+ 82. m xii. **Daniel Clay WEBSTER**, born 12 December 1883, died 24 February 1992.

+ 83. f xiii. **Ella Maude WEBSTER**, born 4 July 1885, died 14 May 1949.

84. f xiv. **Maggie Malinda WEBSTER**, born 19 June 1887 in Kansas. She married **Arthur DOLE**. He was born 1883 in Kansas. Maggie died 22 September 1920, at the age of 33.

+ 85. m xv. **Benjamin Harrison WEBSTER**, born 15 June 1889, died 2 February 1964.

+ 86. m xvi. **Lawrence Lester WEBSTER**, born 9 September 1891, died 16 May 1954.

+ 87. f xvii. **Bertha Jane WEBSTER**, born 22 October 1893, died 11 January

1971.

+ 88. f   xviii.**Minnie Alvina WEBSTER**, born 12 June 1894.
+ 89. f   xix. **Ruth Lorena WEBSTER**, born 12 January 1897, died 25 June 1930.
+ 90. m   xx. **Lee McKinley WEBSTER**, born 5 May 1899, died 9 February 1984.

Nancy also married (1) Reuben AUGUSTINE 1870 in Washington, Iowa. He was the brother of Laura. He was born 1849 in Mt. Pleasant, Henry County, Iowa. Reuben died September 1872 in Talleyrand, Iowa, at the age of 23.

William Daniel Webster was known as "Dan." He is one of the most interesting characters in our line. Dan was six feet tall, light complexion, dark eyes, brown hair, and his occupation was farmer. This physical description was contained in his Civil War pension records.

William Daniel Webster served in the Civil War as a Private in Company K, 44th Regiment, Iowa Infantry from June 1 to September 15, 1864. He enlisted in Davenport, Iowa and was taken to Tennessee probably from Davenport to Memphis by riverboat on the Mississippi River. One document in his pension records said he was deployed near La Grange, Tennessee, which was 30 miles east of Memphis and in Confederate territory. The battle of Shiloh had occurred just east of La Grange on April 6 and 7, 1862. The Union forces under General Ulysses S. Grant were taken by surprise by Confederates under General Albert S.

Johnson. The Union forces suffered more losses than the Confederates but managed to hold the area, which was known thereafter as the "Hornet's Nest." In 1863, the area was a supply point supporting the siege of Vicksburg, Mississippi farther down river. In 1864, the southwestern Tennessee area was still hotly contested. The famous cavalry Confederate General Nathan Bedford Forrest was raiding the Union forces there under General William Tecumseh Sherman, who was using the area as a staging base for his drive into the deep South where he would burn Atlanta.

Southwestern Tennessee is close to the Mississippi River flood plain and at that time was full of swamps and all the unhealthy conditions that go with that type of terrain. For his pension, William Daniel Webster testified that he was at or near La Grange, Tennessee on September 8, 1864 and came down with malaria followed by typhoid fever. Shortly after he was taken sick, he was granted a leave of absence and was returned home and discharged at Davenport, Iowa on September 15, 1864. He was nursed back to health by his first wife, Laura, but suffered from loss of hearing and poor health for the rest of his life because of the diseases.

In the Public Broadcasting System series on the Civil War aired in September, 1990, it said half of all Iowa men of military age served in the Civil War filling 46 regiments in all. A total of 13,001 died: 3,540 in combat, 515 while prisoners of war, and 8,498 of disease. Those figures were typical. When viewed in this context, William Daniel Webster's experience is more understandable.

William Daniel had five children by his first wife, Laura. After she died in 1873, he married Nancy Jane (Jester) Augustine, the widow of Reuben Augustine, Laura's brother. Nancy had one child from her first marriage. Dan and Nancy had another 14 children of their own. Sixteen of their twenty total children were alive when Dan applied for his Civil War pension in 1898. He listed them on the back of the legal sized sheet as required. They filled it up. Dan wrote on the bottom of the list, "Please send a little more paper next time."

Dan and Nancy and their family left Iowa for Kansas about October, 1878. They traveled in covered wagon and arrived in Kansas in time to build a dugout along the Smokey Hill about ten miles northwest of Roxbury before his son, Virgil Franklin Webster, was born on January 31, 1879.

They homesteaded a farm six miles west of Roxbury in 1880. The farm was located in the northeast corner of the section south of the Roxbury-Lindsberg road and west of the Galva road. The family lived in a dugout until a house was built in the spring of 1882 in the southeast corner of the 160-acre plot. About 1888, the family moved to the West Kentuck district about three miles east of Johnstown.

Around 1896, the family moved to a farm near Durham. It was while they were living here that William Daniel lost his left arm. He was riding in a wagon and happened to rest his arm on the end of a shotgun. The shotgun went off accidentally and shattered his arm. He was taken on home and his son, Daniel Clay, aged fourteen, was sent for the doctor. Daniel Clay, who was ill at the time, had to ride bareback on a horse in freezing weather 13 miles to Canton and back. William's arm had to be cut off at the shoulder. Do not feel too sorry for Daniel Clay; he lived to be 108 years old.

They moved to a farm at Dole's Park near Canton and on to Lehigh in 1905. They then moved to a farm north of Canton in 1912 and then to one near Waldick. In 1919, Dan and Nancy bought a house in Canton and lived there until Dan died on April 6, 1927 at the age of 87. Nancy died on April 20,1931 when she was 78.

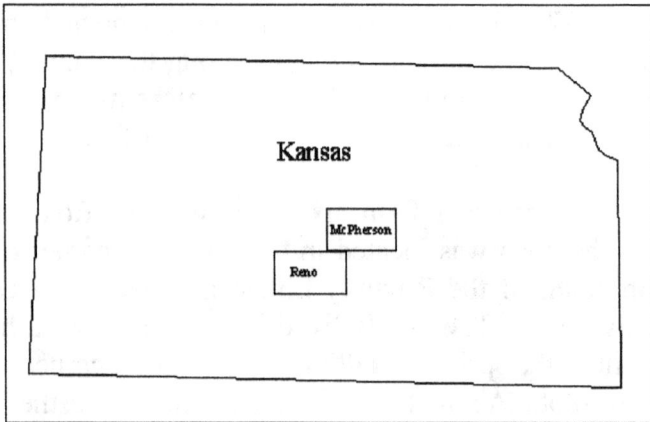

Figure 6 – Map of Kansas showing relevant points.

Aunt Elaine says that Dan and Nancy had over one hundred grandchildren, and that, in their final years at family gatherings, Dan would gather his grandchildren around him and entertain them with stories including some from his past. One such story tells of an Indian squaw stopping by his boyhood home in Seneca County, Ohio to talk to his mother, Mary. The squaw put her baby wrapped in a papoose style back carrier outside the door and went in. A boar gored the baby to death. The squaw buried her child, said something over its grave, and went away.

Aunt Elaine also said that her Grandfather claimed to have some Indian blood, but I have not found any truth to that piece of family lore. It was probably just some of Dan's creative yarn spinning.

Another interesting story concerns Florence Webster, Dan's fifth child by his first wife, Laura. Florence went on the stage. Actors were held in low esteem at the time, and Dan disowned his daughter for sinking so low. Years later she wrote her brother, John, that she would be coming through the Canton Railroad Station and would like to see him. Even though John was married at this time and was living in a home of his own, he did not dare go against his father's wishes and go see his sister. She was never heard of again.

Nancy Jane (Jester) Augustine Webster's Ancestry

Nancy Jane's parents were John Charles "Jesse" and Elizabeth Amanda (White) Jester. They show up very clearly on page 72 of the 1860 Census in Washington County, Iowa. Jesse is a carpenter who was born in Ohio as was his wife, Elizabeth, and their firstborn child, Amanda. Nancy Jane is shown accurately as a six-year-old female born in Iowa. From the records of the children's births, it is evident that they came to Iowa from Ohio between 1847 and 1852.

Figure 7 – William Daniel and Nancy Jane Webster and their children.

Seated left to right: William Daniel, Lee McKinley, Ruth Lorena, and Nancy Jane. Standing front left to right: Maggie, Jonas Marion, Ella Maude, Daniel Clay, Bertha Jane, Minnie Alvina, and Mary Etta. Standing in back from left to right: Howard Lincoln, Benjamin Harrison, Lawrence Lester, and Virgil Franklin.
(Circa 1910)

However, an examination of Jesters in Ohio does not clearly show this family. Perhaps they were in a larger household there. Most of the Jesters were concentrated in the southwestern quadrant of Ohio. Their 1850 Census records show many of the older Jester family members were born in Delaware.

Delaware is noted for being settled in large measure by Swedish people in Colonial times. The 1800 Census shows many Jesters in Delaware. Surnames with the "ster" suffix like Jester and Webster are Teutonic and Scandinavian in origin. Therefore, although this is only conjecture, it seems likely that our Jesters were Swedish people who first settled in Delaware and then moved west.

- - - - - - - - - - -

26. M. Lafayette³ WEBSTER (4.Mary², 1.Jacob¹) was born 1 September 1842 in Seneca County, Ohio. He was the son of John H. WEBSTER and Mary Magdalene MOOMEY. M. Lafayette died about 1923 in California. He married **Mary Ann ARMSTRONG**. She was born 1846 in Seneca County, Ohio.

They had 8 children:

91. f i. **Francis Ellen WEBSTER**, born 4 October 1863. She married **Clarence ANDERSON**. Francis died 9 March 1951, at the age of 87.

92. f ii. **Minnie Moselle WEBSTER**, born 12 March 1869. She married **John C. CROSS**. Minnie died

23 March 1942, at the age of 73.

93. f iii. **Jennie Orilla WEBSTER**, born 1871, died in infancy May 1872.

94. f iv. **Laura May WEBSTER**, born 18 October 1874. She married **Fred H. CROW**. Laura died 23 January 1965, at the age of 90.

95. m v. **Charles Sylvester WEBSTER**, born 2 March 1876. He married **Jennie Mae PATTERSON**. Charles died after 1972.

96. m vi. **Clayton Emery WEBSTER**, born October 1878, died in childhood 7 May 1889, at the age of 10.

97. f vii. **Josephine Maude WEBSTER**, born 15 October 1880. She married **Elmer E. YODER**. Josephine died after 1972.

98. m viii. **Wesley Blaine WEBSTER**, born 15 August 1884. He married **Emma DURIAN**.

- - - - - - - - - -

29. **Nancy³ WEBSTER** (4.Mary², 1.Jacob¹) was born 21 June 1849 in Seneca County, Ohio. She was the daughter of John H. WEBSTER and Mary Magdalene MOOMEY. Nancy died 29 January 1918 in Windham, Iowa, at the age of 68. She married **Abraham LEWIS**. He was born 1845 in Seneca County, Ohio.

They had 1 child:

99. m i. **Frank LEWIS**.

- - - - - - - - - - -

30. Frehling Sylvester³ WEBSTER (4.Mary², 1.Jacob¹) was born 19 December 1851 in Iowa City, Johnson County, Iowa. He was the son of John H. WEBSTER and Mary Magdalene MOOMEY. Frehling died 24 January 1929 in Greene Twp., Iowa County, Iowa, at the age of 77, and was buried in Oakland Cemetery, Iowa City, Johnson County, Iowa. He married **Florence Rowena ANDERSON** 1883 in Johnson County, Iowa. She was born 1855 in Iowa City, Johnson County, Iowa.

They had 3 children:

100.	f	i.	**Ethel May WEBSTER**, born 26 October 1884. She married **Daniel E. YODER**. Ethel died 29 April 1932, at the age of 47.
101.	m	ii.	**Elmer Earl WEBSTER**, born 6 September 1886. He married **Mamie Mae COX**.
+ 102.	m	iii.	**Arthur H. WEBSTER**, born 8 January 1888, died 29 April 1939.

After his father's death, Frehling continued with the Webster family business of brick and tile factory and saw mill.

- - - - - - - - - - -

44. Minerva "Minnie"³ DIXON (8.Catherine², 1.Jacob¹) was born 18 March 1865 in Bloomington, McLean County, Illinois. She was the daughter of William A. DIXON and Catherine MOOMEY. Minerva died 8 March 1937 in Cheyenne, Laramie County, Wyoming, at the age of 72. 1870 Federal Census, Union Township, Wayne County, Iowa, p.

362.   She   married   **Cyrus   Richmond   FENWICK**
20 December 1882 in Perry, Dallas County, Iowa. He was
born 30 October 1860 in What Cheer, Keokuk County, Iowa.
Cyrus died 9 August 1935 in Cheyenne, Laramie County,
Wyoming, at the age of 74.

They had 4 children:

+ 103. m   i.   **Willis Raymond FENWICK**, born 2 July
1884, died 18 May 1962.
+ 104. m   ii.   **Leslie Earle FENWICK**, born 2 August
1886, died April 1980.
+ 105. f   iii.   **Mabel   Fern   FENWICK**,   born
22 September 1889, died 1935.
+ 106. f   iv.   **Vay Inel FENWICK**, born 17 November
1892, died 19 March 1971.

Cyrus' extended Fenwick family lived in Oskaloosa,
Mahaska, Iowa, from 1870, until Mr. and Mrs. James
Ephriam Fenwick (parents of Cyrus) passed on in between
1898-1905. There is a history book of the town with the
Fenwicks being part of the Methodist Church movement.
James served in the American/Mexican War and applied for a
pension in 1900. He made his "X" mark on the application
co-signed by his sons, James, Jr. and John Fenwick.

Most of the Fenwick family stayed in Iowa for many years
with at least two of the sons becoming ministers. Both Cyrus
and Minnie were ordained ministers serving in Iowa until the
early 1900's. They moved to Wyoming where they served as
ministers for many years. According to one Wyoming
history, "Mrs. Minnie Dixon Fenwick and Reverend Cyrus
Fenwick have had a life that has been crowded with deeds
and services to others. Mrs. Fenwick looks back when she

carried the banner of the Gospel into the new fields and started new preaching circuits in a newly opened land." She served as President of the Woman's Christian Temperance Union for several years traveling through the Wyoming area "spreading the word" against bootlegging. In addition to serving the ministry, Cyrus Fenwick was a carpenter and photographer. He organized the First Masonic Order in Burns, Wyoming.

CHAPTER 4

GENERATION NO. 4

The fourth generation of Jacob and Mary Moomey's family were their great grandchildren. They lived at the turn of the century and into the twentieth century. During this period, they experienced the Industrial Revolution and saw their lives transformed by modern innovations, such as the automobile, the airplane, indoor plumbing, the electric light, and motion pictures. They also saw America participate in two world wars of unprecedented scale and fury. They suffered the Great Depression of the 1930s as well.

60. Clarence Mitchell[4] MOOMEY (20.Henry[3], 3.John[2], 1.Jacob[1]) was born 29 March 1873 in Osceola, Clarke County, Iowa. He was the son of Henry Washington MOOMEY and Clarinda C. BONHAM. Clarence died 9 April 1950 in Osceola, Clarke County, Iowa, at the age of 77, and was buried in Maple Hill Cemetery, Osceola, Clarke County, Iowa. He married **Lelah Eunice ARNOLD** 1 November 1891 in Greenbay Township, Clarke County, Iowa. She was born 20 September 1876 in Clarke County, Iowa. She was the daughter of Francis ARNOLD and Laura JOHNSON. Lelah died 22 July 1963 in Osceola, Clarke County, Iowa, at the age of 86, and was buried in Maple Hill Cemetery, Osceola, Clarke County, Iowa.

They had 13 children:

107. f   i.   **Grace Marlee MOOMEY**, born 29 August 1892 in Clarke County, Iowa. She married **Edson F.**

SMITH 28 October 1911 in Clarke County, Iowa. Grace died 24 February 1945 in Clarke County, Iowa, at the age of 52, and was buried in Maple Hill Cemetery, Osceola, Clarke County, Iowa.

108. m ii. **Carl Henry MOOMEY**, born 13 September 1894 in Clarke County, Iowa. He married **Maude LANGFITT** 13 August 1914 in Clarke County, Iowa. Carl died 5 June 1978 in Clarke County, Iowa, at the age of 83, and was buried in Maple Hill Cemetery, Osceola, Clarke County, Iowa.

109. m iii. **Gerald Burr MOOMEY**, born 4 July 1897 in Washington, Johnson County, Iowa. He married (1) **Edith MILER**. She was born 1897. Edith died 1923, at the age of 26. Gerald married (2) **Lorraine EGAR** 24 January 1941. Gerald died 1968 in Decatur County, Iowa, at the age of 70, and was buried in Kellerton Cemetery.

110. m iv. **Harry Bryan MOOMEY**, born 10 September 1899 in Washington, Johnson County, Iowa, died 2 July 1921 in Clarke County, Iowa, at the age of 21, and was buried in

Fremont Cemetery.

111. f v. **Eithel Pauline MOOMEY**, born 2 September 1902 in Washington, Johnson County, Iowa.

112. m vi. **Echo Lewis MOOMEY**, born 27 September 1905 in Washington, Johnson County, Iowa, died in infancy 25 August 1907 in Washington, Johnson County, Iowa, and was buried in Frank Pierce Cemetery, Johnson County, Iowa.

113. f vii. **Lelah Waunita MOOMEY**, born 7 January 1908 in Washington, Johnson County, Iowa. She married **Willard Warren CARPER** 20 May 1933 in Washington, Johnson County, Iowa. Lelah died 9 October 1985 in Osceola, Clarke County, Iowa, at the age of 77.

114. f viii. **Violet Wanda MOOMEY**, born 7 January 1908 in Washington, Johnson County, Iowa. She married **Lee DELANEY**. Lee died August 1984. Violet died 7 February 1984 in Creston, Iowa, at the age of 76, and was buried in Creston Cemetery, Creston, Iowa.

115. f ix. **Hazel Irene MOOMEY**, born 18 September 1910 in Clarke

County, Iowa, died in infancy 10 January 1911 in Clarke County, Iowa, and was buried in Fremont Cemetery.

116. f   x.   **Hildreth MOOMEY**, born 18 September 1910 in Clarke County, Iowa, died in infancy 18 September 1910 in Clarke County, Iowa, and was buried in Fremont Cemetery.

117. f   xi.   **Nellie Arline MOOMEY**, born 17 April 1912 in Clarke County, Iowa. She married **Lloyd B. ZEPP**. Nellie died 13 May 1984 in Des Moines, Iowa, at the age of 72, and was buried in Maple Hill Cemetery, Osceola, Clarke County, Iowa.

118. m   xii.   **Paul MOOMEY**, born 17 April 1912 in Clarke County, Iowa, died in infancy 17 April 1912 in Clarke County, Iowa, and was buried in Fremont Cemetery.

+ 119. m   xiii.   **Donald William MOOMEY**, born 21 May 1915.

Clarence was a farmer and affiliated with the Christian Church. For some years before their deaths, Clarence and Lelah lived in their son Donald's household.

- - - - - - - - - -

62. Bruce[4] MOOMEY (21.LeRoy[3], 3.John[2], 1.Jacob[1]) was born 14 July 1876. He was the son of LeRoy MOOMEY and Cora FRY. Bruce died 1951, at the age of 74. He married **Ostia BROWN** 5 June 1901.

They had 1 child:

120. m   i.   **LaMont MOOMEY**.

Bruce was a photographer in Wellmon, Iowa. He later moved to California in the Los Angeles area.

- - - - - - - - - - -

72. William Wesley[4] WEBSTER (25.William[3], 4.Mary[2], 1.Jacob[1]) was born 7 March 1863 in Indian County, Iowa. He was the son of William Daniel WEBSTER and Laura AUGUSTINE. William died 25 October 1933, at the age of 70. He married **Wilemina Johanna "Minnie" CLUDAS**.

They had 2 children:

121. m   i.   **Howard WEBSTER**.

+ 122. m   ii.   **Stanley Ross WEBSTER**, born 8 June 1886, died 5 February 1960.

William was a blacksmith in Canton, Kansas.

- - - - - - - - - - -

73. Almyra May[4] WEBSTER (25.William[3], 4.Mary[2], 1.Jacob[1]) was born 8 September 1865. She was the daughter of William Daniel WEBSTER and Laura AUGUSTINE. She married **William MANUELS**.

They had 3 children:

123. f   i.   **Pearl MANUELS**.

124. m ii. **William MANUELS.**
125. f iii. **Edith MANUELS.**

- - - - - - - - - - -

74. John Ellsworth[4] WEBSTER (25.William[3], 4.Mary[2], 1.Jacob[1]) was born 6 April 1869. He was the son of William Daniel WEBSTER and Laura AUGUSTINE. John died 21 March 1941, at the age of 71. He married **Maggie GABLE.**

They had 3 children:
126. m i. **Arthur WEBSTER.**
127. f ii. **Gertrude WEBSTER.**
128. m iii. **John Raymond WEBSTER.**

- - - - - - - - - - -

77. Marion Jonas[4] WEBSTER (25.William[3], 4.Mary[2], 1.Jacob[1]) was born 21 December 1874 in Iowa. He was the son of William Daniel WEBSTER and Nancy Jane JESTER. Marion died 21 October 1932, at the age of 57. He married **Lida LEE**. She was born 1878 in Iowa.

They had 1 child:
129. m i. **Marrium WEBSTER.**

- - - - - - - - - - -

79. Mary Etta[4] WEBSTER (25.William[3], 4.Mary[2], 1.Jacob[1]) was born 16 March 1877 in Iowa. She was the daughter of William Daniel WEBSTER and Nancy Jane JESTER. Mary died in California. She married **Carl**

48

GIDDINGS. He was born 1873 in Iowa.

They had 5 children:

130.	m	i.	**Chester GIDDINGS.**
131.	f	ii.	**Edna GIDDINGS.**
132.	f	iii.	**Mildred GIDDINGS.**
133.	f	iv.	**Marion GIDDINGS.**
134.	f	v.	**Clarice GIDDINGS.**

- - - - - - - - - -

80. Virgil Franklin[4] WEBSTER (25.William[3], 4.Mary[2], 1.Jacob[1]) was born 31 January 1879 in near Lindsburg, McPherson County, Kansas. He was the son of William Daniel WEBSTER and Nancy Jane JESTER. Virgil died 25 July 1962 in Canton, McPherson County, Kansas, at the age of 83. He married **Pearl H. WHITTENBERG** 1 March 1905 in Canton, McPherson County, Kansas. She was born 1883 in Kansas.

They had 6 children:

135.	m	i.	**Milton WEBSTER.**
136.	f	ii.	**Violet WEBSTER.**
137.	f	iii.	**Laverne WEBSTER.**
138.	m	iv.	**Kenneth WEBSTER.**
139.	f	v.	**Lucille WEBSTER.**
140.	f	vi.	**Dorothy WEBSTER.**

- - - - - - - - - -

81. Howard Lincoln[4] WEBSTER (25.William[3], 4.Mary[2], 1.Jacob[1]) was born 16 October 1881 in near Lindsburg, McPherson County, Kansas. He was the son of William

Daniel WEBSTER and Nancy Jane JESTER. Howard died 27 November 1969 in El Dorado, Butler County, Kansas, at the age of 88. He married **Elizabeth "Bessy" WINING** 27 April 1906 in El Dorado, Butler County, Kansas. She was born 19 October 1887 in Carbon Cliff, Rock Island County, Illinois. She was the daughter of William Shippen WINING and Mary Anna FULLER. Elizabeth died 29 October 1942 in Winfield, Cowley County, Kansas, at the age of 55, and was buried in Canton Cemetery, McPherson County, Kansas.

They had 7 children:

+ 141. m i. **Gerald WEBSTER**, born 13 October 1907, died 6 April 1990.

+ 142. m ii. **William Wining WEBSTER**, born 19 March 1910.

143. f iii. **Madlyn E. WEBSTER**, born 10 June 1912, died in childhood 7 August 1914, at the age of 2, and was buried in Canton Cemetery, McPherson County, Kansas.

144. f iv. **M. Marjorie WEBSTER**, born 26 March 1915 in Canton, McPherson County, Kansas. She married **Paul COX** 9 September 1930.

+ 145. f v. **Maxine D. WEBSTER**, born 17 November 1917.

+ 146. f vi. **Pauline WEBSTER**, born 1 September 1920.

+ 147. f vii. **Norma Geraldine WEBSTER**, born 28 May 1927.

- - - - - - - - - -

82. Daniel Clay[4] WEBSTER (25.William[3], 4.Mary[2], 1.Jacob[1]) was born 12 December 1883 in Crazy Ridge, McPherson County, Kansas. He was the son of William Daniel WEBSTER and Nancy Jane JESTER. Daniel died 24 February 1992 in Roxbury, Kansas, at the age of **108**. He married **Lillian KEEFER** 8 November 1913. She was born 29 July 1891 in Admire, Kansas. She was the daughter of John Grant KEEFER and Alice BAXTER. Lillian died 5 August 1965 in Lindsberg, Kansas, at the age of 74.

They had 7 children:

+ 148. m   i.   **Everett Winston WEBSTER**, born 28 December 1914.

+ 149. m   ii.   **Wendell Sherwood WEBSTER**, born 27 March 1916.

+ 150. f   iii.   **Wilma Allene WEBSTER**, born 5 December 1918.

+ 151. m   iv.   **Warren Frances WEBSTER**, born 20 March 1923.

+ 152. m   v.   **Ronald Daniel WEBSTER**, born 14 November 1925.

+ 153. f   vi.   **Alice Jane WEBSTER**, born 4 February 1928.

+ 154. f   vii.   **Patricia Lillian WEBSTER**, born 24 March 1931, died 6 November 1979.

- - - - - - - - - -

83. Ella Maude[4] WEBSTER (25.William[3], 4.Mary[2], 1.Jacob[1]) was born 4 July 1885 in Kansas. She was the daughter of William Daniel WEBSTER and Nancy Jane JESTER. Ella died 14 May 1949, at the age of 63. She married **Revillow ROYCE**. He was born 1881 in Kansas.

They had 2 children:

155. m i. **Harold ROYCE.**
156. f ii. **Marcellas ROYCE.**

- - - - - - - - - -

85. Benjamin Harrison[4] WEBSTER (25.William[3], 4.Mary[2], 1.Jacob[1]) was born 15 June 1889 in Lindsberg, McPherson County, Kansas. He was the son of William Daniel WEBSTER and Nancy Jane JESTER. Benjamin died 2 February 1964 in Great Bend, Barton County, Kansas, at the age of 74, and was buried 6 February 1964 in Canton, McPherson County, Kansas. He married **Laveta Fern OLDFIELD** 16 May 1911 in Hutchinson, Reno County, Kansas. She was born 8 August 1890 in Canton, McPherson County, Kansas. She was the daughter of Alonzo David OLDFIELD and Clara Myrtes KIRBY. Laveta died 6 March 1971 in Lyons, Rice County, Kansas, at the age of 80, and was buried 10 March 1971 in Canton, McPherson County, Kansas.[13]

They had 6 children:

+ 157. m i. **Reginald Dale WEBSTER,** born 26 August 1911, died 2 July 1965.
+ 158. f ii. **Elaine Maxine WEBSTER,** born 24 February 1914.
+ 159. f iii. **Virginia Enola WEBSTER,** born

---

[13] Kansas Death Certificate #71 004793.

6 August 1916, died 5 July 1976.

160. f   iv. **Inez Ruth WEBSTER**, born 9 September 1918 in Canton, McPherson County, Kansas. She married (1) **Ralph WATSON** 1937 in Alma, Nebraska. He was born 14 August 1909 in Haven, Kansas. Ralph died 1972 in Lyons, Kansas, at the age of 62. Inez married (2) **Noah Eugene RIDER** 14 August 1974 in Abilene, Kansas. He was born 25 September 1924 in Salina, Kansas.

+ 161. m   v. **Randall Harry WEBSTER**, born 31 March 1923, died 15 June 1994.

+ 162. m   vi. **Bob Rex Alvin WEBSTER**, born 29 October 1925.

My Grandmother Webster, Laveta Fern, was a very sweet lady. One vivid memory of her was her singing "Amazing Grace" while hanging clothes out to dry.

As you can see it the following picture, she had wonderful naturally curly, wavy hair that seemed to be a prominent Oldfield feature. I have that Oldfield hair and used to dislike it as unmanageable. Now, I appreciate it as a gift from my grandmother and let it curl and wave as it wants instead of trying to straighten it.

She and my Grandfather Harry Webster lived in a large two story white wood frame house on the east side of the small farm town of Canton in central Kansas. In their last years together, they lived in a small apartment in nearby Lyons, Kansas, close to my Aunts Ruth and Virginia who primarily assisted them. When my Grandfather died in 1964, Grandma went into an old peoples' home in Lyons until her death in 1971.

The cause of her death was cerebral arteriosclerosis.

Figure 8
Laveta Fern Oldfield
(Circa 1911)

Grandfather Harry was a great story teller and comedian. He used to entertain his grandchildren by imitating Charlie Chaplin. He did the "Little Tramp" walk very well.

Benjamin Harrison "Harry" Webster's Obituary in the Canton Pilot of 2 February 1964:

"A retired automobile dealer and salesman died Sunday, February 2, 1964, at St. Rose Hospital, Great Bend. He had been in failing health for about a year.

Born on a farm near Lindsborg June 15, 1889, "Harry", as he was popularly known, spent many years of his life in the Roxbury, Gypsum, and Lindsborg communities.

At one time he owned and operated a Ford dealership in Canton at the location now occupied by Friendly Chevrolet. For about ten years he has been in the automobile business in Lyons. "

Harry died of lung problems from a lifelong smoking habit. I remember seeing him on his deathbed gasping for breath and making a loud death rattle. It is too bad that this memory is the last one I have of him, because I thought he was an adorable man in many ways.

- - - - - - - - - -

86. Lawrence Lester[4] WEBSTER (25.William[3], 4.Mary[2], 1.Jacob[1]) was born 9 September 1891 in Canton, McPherson

County, Kansas. He was the son of William Daniel WEBSTER and Nancy Jane JESTER. Lawrence died 16 May 1954 in El Dorado, Butler County, Kansas, at the age of 62, and was buried 18 May 1954 in Canton Cemetery, McPherson County, Kansas.[14] He married **Nora OLLENBERGER**. She was born 1895 in Canton, McPherson County, Kansas.

They had 5 children:

163.	m	i.	**Earl WEBSTER.**
164.	m	ii.	**Emerson WEBSTER.**
165.	f	iii.	**Evelyn WEBSTER.**
166.	f	iv.	**Velma WEBSTER.**
167.	m	v.	**Lester WEBSTER.**

- - - - - - - - - -

87. Bertha Jane[4] WEBSTER (25.William[3], 4.Mary[2], 1.Jacob[1]) was born 22 October 1893 in Durham, Kansas. She was the daughter of William Daniel WEBSTER and Nancy Jane JESTER. Bertha died 11 January 1971 in Marion County, Kansas, at the age of 77, and was buried in Mennonite Cemetery, Hillsboro, Kansas. She married **John F. UNRUH**. He was born 12 April 1891 in Marion County, Kansas. He was the son of John J. UNRUH and Mary FRIESEN. John died 4 June 1974 in Marion County, Kansas, at the age of 83, and was buried in Mennonite Cemetery, Hillsboro, Kansas.

They had 7 children:

+ 168. m   i.   **Elman J. UNRUH**, born 31 January 1917.

---

[14] Funeral program, The Danielson-Ball Chapel.

+ 169. f   ii.   **Clarice Elsie UNRUH**, born 28 April 1918.

+ 170. m   iii.   **Louis Daniel UNRUH**, born 24 July 1919.

171. m   iv.   **Harold Marvin UNRUH**, born 27 November 1922 in Marion County, Kansas. He married **Nelva Ruth HOCH** 21 November 1945.

+ 172. f   v.   **Erma Mae UNRUH**, born 12 September 1928.

+ 173. f   vi.   **Doris Jane UNRUH**, born 18 August 1932.

+ 174. m   vii.   **Jonas Boyd UNRUH**, born 28 April 1934.

- - - - - - - - - -

88. Minnie Alvina[4] WEBSTER (25.William[3], 4.Mary[2], 1.Jacob[1]) was born 12 June 1894 in Kansas. She is the daughter of William Daniel WEBSTER and Nancy Jane JESTER. She married **Alban SWALLANDER**. He was born 1890 in Kansas.

They had 1 child:

175. f   i.   **Delores Lamar SWALLANDER**.

- - - - - - - - - -

89. Ruth Lorena[4] WEBSTER (25.William[3], 4.Mary[2], 1.Jacob[1]) was born 12 January 1897 in Kansas. She was the daughter of William Daniel WEBSTER and Nancy Jane JESTER. Ruth died 25 June 1930, at the age of 33. She married **Herman HACKLER**. He was born 1893 in Kansas.

They had 1 child:

176.   f   i.   **Nona Mae HACKLER**.

- - - - - - - - - - -

90. Lee McKinley[4] WEBSTER (25.William[3], 4.Mary[2], 1.Jacob[1]) was born 5 May 1899 in Kansas. He was the son of William Daniel WEBSTER and Nancy Jane JESTER. Lee died 9 February 1984 in Valley Center, Sedgwick County, Kansas, at the age of 84. He married **Waneta FULLENWITER**. She was born 1903 in <Kansas>.

They had 2 children:

177.   m   i.   **William WEBSTER**.
178.   m   ii. **Robert WEBSTER**.

- - - - - - - - - - -

76. Clarence B.[4] AUGUSTINE (stepchild of 25.William[3], 4.Mary[2], 1.Jacob[1]). He was the son of Reuben AUGUSTINE and Nancy Jane JESTER. He married **Retta ALLEN**.

They had 6 children:

179.   m   i.   **Chester AUGUSTINE**.
180.   f   ii.   **Viva AUGUSTINE**.
181.   f   iii. **Ruth AUGUSTINE**.
182.   f   iv.   **Mattie AUGUSTINE**.
183.   m   v.   **Fred AUGUSTINE**.
184.   m   vi.   **Ben AUGUSTINE**.

- - - - - - - - - - -

102. Arthur H.[4] WEBSTER (30.Frehling[3], 4.Mary[2],

1.Jacob[1]) was born 8 January 1888 in Iowa County, Iowa. He was the son of Frehling Sylvester WEBSTER and Florence Rowena ANDERSON. Arthur died 29 April 1939 in Iowa City, Iowa, at the age of 51. He married **Blanche Bernice BUCK** 14 September 1911 in Johnson County, Iowa. She was born 19 November 1891 in Johnson County, Iowa. Blanche died 19 January 1965 in Iowa City, Iowa, at the age of 73.

They had 1 child:

+ 185. m   i.   **Howard Emerson WEBSTER**, born 20 November 1913, died 21 July 1991.

- - - - - - - - - - -

103. Willis Raymond[4] FENWICK (44.Minerva[3], 8.Catherine[2], 1.Jacob[1]) was born 2 July 1884 in Moline, Rock Island County, Illinois. He was the son of Cyrus Richmond FENWICK and Minerva "Minnie" DIXON. Willis died 18 May 1962 in San Francisco, California, at the age of 77. He married **Ida Victoria HOCUM**; they divorced. She was born 1886.

They had 4 children:

186. m   i.   **Kenneth Richmond FENWICK**, born 1910. He married **Alice Mae IZETT**.

187. m   ii.   **Willis Henry FENWICK**, born 1910. He married **Ruth NELSON**.

188. m   iii.   **Leslie FENWICK**, born 1912. He married **Dorothy OLSON**.

189. f   iv.   **Lucille Maurine FENWICK**, born 1919.

She married **Donald KANE**.

Willis Raymond Fenwick married Ida Victoria Hocum, who was from a Swedish family who farmed in the Mason City, Iowa, area. Willis Raymond worked in Wyoming for a short time before moving to Golden, Colorado, where he and Ida raised their family. She was a housekeeper working for her own family as well as for other families. Raymond went from Golden to Denver weekly working for the tramway system. He left the family when the boys were in their late teens and moved to California where he was a security guard marrying twice more. All four of their children (Ken, Willis, Les and Lucille) made successes of their lives bringing 9 grandchildren and many great grandchildren into the Fenwick family.

- - - - - - - - - -

104. Leslie Earle[4] FENWICK (44.Minerva[3], 8.Catherine[2], 1.Jacob[1]) was born 2 August 1886 in Oskaloosa, Mahaska County, Iowa. He was the son of Cyrus Richmond FENWICK and Minerva "Minnie" DIXON. Leslie died April 1980 in Colorado Springs, El Paso County, Colorado, at the age of 93. He married **Ora Lena RABAR**. She was born 1889.

They had 2 children:
190. m i. **Jack Elwood FENWICK**.
191. m ii. **Robert Lee FENWICK**.

Leslie Earle Fenwick was printer and worked in the newspaper business all his life. He must have served in some form of service as he died in a Veteran's home.

- - - - - - - - - -

105. Mabel Fern[4] FENWICK (44.Minerva[3], 8.Catherine[2], 1.Jacob[1]) was born 22 September 1889 in Oskaloosa, Mahaska County, Iowa. She was the daughter of Cyrus Richmond FENWICK and Minerva "Minnie" DIXON. Mabel died 1935 in Greybull, Big Horn County, Wyoming, at the age of 45. She married **Stanley K. MARKLEY** 1914 in Bruns/Luther, Laramie County, Wyoming. He was born 1886.

They had 2 children:

192. f   i.   **Dorothy Inel MARKLEY**, born 1914.
193. f   ii.   **Elma Leona MARKLEY**, born 1917. She married **Robert GRANDJEAN**.

- - - - - - - - - -

106. Vay Inel[4] FENWICK (44.Minerva[3], 8.Catherine[2], 1.Jacob[1]) was born 17 November 1892 in Oskaloosa, Mahaska County, Iowa. She was the daughter of Cyrus Richmond FENWICK and Minerva "Minnie" DIXON. Vay died 19 March 1971 in Cheyenne, Laramie County, Wyoming, at the age of 78. She married **Arleigh J. COOPER** 17 April 1915 in Cheyenne, Laramie County, Wyoming. He was born 1893.

They had 4 children:

194. f   i.   **Genevieve Lorraine COOPER**, born 1916. She married **Earl Luther FARR**.

195. m   ii.   **Gerald Winston COOPER**, born 1925. He married **Bonita F. LANNING**.

196. f   iii. **Beth COOPER**, born 1926. She married **John James BERRY**. Beth wrote a family history of the Cooper and Fenwick families.

197. f   iv.   **Dorothy Dee COOPER**, born 1946. She married **Roger Allen SIMMONS**.

Both Vay Inel Fenwick and Mabel Fern Fenwick were teachers having received their teaching certificates from the normal training school in Burns, Wyoming. They   stayed with families in the area where they taught. They rode to and from school on horseback.

CHAPTER 5

GENERATION NO. 5

The fifth generation consists of the great great grandchildren of Jacob and Mary Moomey. They lived mainly in the first half of the twentieth century. Many of them came off the farms to live in the towns and cities and to work in the factories. They suffered through the financial problems of the Great Depression. They participated in the industrialization of the workforce and in two world wars and the Korean War as well. They saw air travel become common and witnessed our first steps into space and the landing on the moon.

119. Donald William[5] MOOMEY (60.Clarence[4], 20.Henry[3], 3.John[2], 1.Jacob[1]) was born 21 May 1915 in Clarke County, Iowa. He is the son of Clarence Mitchell MOOMEY and Lelah Eunice ARNOLD. Donald died, and was buried in Maple Hill Cemetery, Osceola, Clarke County, Iowa. He married **Leota Mae McBROOM** 14 August 1937 in Creston, Iowa. She was born 16 April 1921 in Jamison, Clarke County, Iowa.

They had 2 children:

198. f   i.   **Joyce Rae MOOMEY**, born 1 March 1942 in Osceola, Clarke County, Iowa. She married **Russell E. FISHER** 8 September 1961 in Orlando, Florida; they divorced.

+ 199. m   ii.   **Donald Franklin MOOMEY**, born 3 April 1947.

- - - - - - - - - - -

122. Stanley Ross^5 WEBSTER (72.William^4, 25.William^3, 4.Mary^2, 1.Jacob^1) was born 8 June 1886 in Ness County, Kansas. He was the son of William Wesley WEBSTER and Wilemina Johanna "Minnie" CLUDAS. Stanley died 5 February 1960, at the age of 73. He married **Mabel A. SPURRIER** 26 June 1907. She was born 1 August 1879 in Kent, Taylor County, Iowa. She was the daughter of Samuel Franklin SPURRIER and Margaret Eleanor WICKHAM. Mabel died 28 January 1959 in Glendale, Los Angeles County, California, at the age of 79.

They had 5 children:

200. m i. **Stanton Frank WEBSTER**, born 12 June 1908 in McPherson, McPherson County, Kansas, died in infancy 1909 in McPherson, McPherson County, Kansas.

201. f ii. **Loraine Eleanor WEBSTER**, born 12 July 1908 in McPherson, McPherson County, Kansas.

+ 202. m iii. **William Eugene WEBSTER**, born 28 February 1911, died 12 May 1969.

203. m iv. **James WEBSTER**, born 13 August 1916 in McPherson County, Kansas. He married **Geraldine GRIFFITH** 27 February 1941. James died 5 January 1997 in San Bernardino, California, at the age of 80.

204. f v. **Geraldine Marilyn WEBSTER**, born 21 October 1918 in Kansas, died

15 May 1964, at the age of 45.

- - - - - - - - - - -

141. Gerald⁵ WEBSTER (81.Howard⁴, 25.William³, 4.Mary², 1.Jacob¹) was born 13 October 1907 in Canton, Kansas. He was the son of Howard Lincoln WEBSTER and Elizabeth "Bessy" WINING. Gerald died 6 April 1990 in Canton, Kansas, at the age of 82. He married **June FULLER.**

They had 8 children:

205.	m	i.	**Forrest WEBSTER.**
206.	m	ii.	**Enos WEBSTER.**
207.	m	iii.	**Larry WEBSTER.**
208.	f	iv.	**Gloria WEBSTER.** She married _____ **STUBBS.**
209.	f	v.	**Phyllis WEBSTER.** She married _____ **Metcalf-CARNER.**
210.	f	vi.	**Selma WEBSTER.** She married _____ **BRICKLE.**
211.	f	vii.	**Lota WEBSTER.** She married _____ **MILLER.**
212.	f	viii.	**Mary WEBSTER.** She married _____ **GRUVER.**

- - - - - - - - - - -

142. William Wining⁵ WEBSTER (81.Howard⁴, 25.William³, 4.Mary², 1.Jacob¹) was born 19 March 1910 in Canton, Kansas. He is the son of Howard Lincoln WEBSTER and Elizabeth "Bessy" WINING. He married **Kathryn HOLIDAY.**

They had 2 children:
213.   m   i.   **Billy WEBSTER**, born 3 October.
214.   m   ii.   **Thomas WEBSTER**, born 28 May.

- - - - - - - - - - -

145. Maxine D.[5] **WEBSTER** (81.Howard[4], 25.William[3], 4.Mary[2], 1.Jacob[1]) was born 17 November 1917 in Gypsum, McPherson County, Kansas. She is the daughter of Howard Lincoln WEBSTER and Elizabeth "Bessy" WINING. She married **Gene CAGLE**.
They had 2 children:
215.   m   i.   **Mickey   CAGLE**,   born   30 November 1940.
216.   m   ii.   **Rexter   Vernon   CAGLE**,   born 14 February 1942.

- - - - - - - - - -

146. Pauline[5] **WEBSTER** (81.Howard[4], 25.William[3], 4.Mary[2], 1.Jacob[1]) was born 1 September 1920 in Midian, Butler County, Kansas. She is the daughter of Howard Lincoln WEBSTER and Elizabeth "Bessy" WINING. She married **N. A. JOHNSTON**.
They had 1 child:
217.   m   i.   **Robert   Stanton   JOHNSTON**,   born 6 October.

- - - - - - - - - -

147.   Norma   Geraldine[5] **WEBSTER** (81.Howard[4],

25.William³, 4.Mary², 1.Jacob¹) was born 28 May 1927 in Midian, Butler County, Kansas. She is the daughter of Howard Lincoln WEBSTER and Elizabeth "Bessy" WINING. She married **Edwin R. KING** 1942.

They had 2 children:
218.   m   i.   **Edwin KING**, born 29 October .
219.   m   ii.   **Ernest KING**, born 29 October .

- - - - - - - - - -

148.   Everett   Winston⁵   WEBSTER   (82.Daniel⁴, 25.William³, 4.Mary², 1.Jacob¹) was born 28 December 1914. He is the son of Daniel Clay WEBSTER and Lillian KEEFER.   He married (1) **Elizabeth [————?————]** 13 April 1949.

They had 1 child:
220.   m   i.   **Edward   Daniel   WEBSTER**,   born 19 December 1949. He married **Ann   BERNARDO**   10 August 1974.

Everett married (2) **Gretel NAHR** 11 February 1960. Gretel died July 1967.

No children have yet been identified.

Everett married (3) **Cacilia MAYER** 7 March 1968. She was born 28 January 1934.

No children have yet been identified.

- - - - - - - - - -

149. Wendell Sherwood[5] WEBSTER (82.Daniel[4], 25.William[3], 4.Mary[2], 1.Jacob[1]) was born 27 March 1916. He is the son of Daniel Clay WEBSTER and Lillian KEEFER. He married **Dorothy KARLEY** 18 June 1942. She was born 22 February 1920.

They had 2 children:

+ 221. f   i.   **Barbara Kay WEBSTER**, born 11 July 1944.

222. f   ii.   **Wendy Karleen WEBSTER**, born 22 May 1949. She married **Randy HURST** 26 July 1970. He was born 3 May 1945.

- - - - - - - - - -

150. Wilma Allene[5] WEBSTER (82.Daniel[4], 25.William[3], 4.Mary[2], 1.Jacob[1]) was born 5 December 1918. She is the daughter of Daniel Clay WEBSTER and Lillian KEEFER. She married **George HURCH** 11 October 1934. He was born 14 December 1905. George died 11 May 1967, at the age of 61.

They had 8 children:

+ 223. m   i.   **Gerald Gene HURCH**, born 16 August 1936.

+ 224. m   ii.   **Charles Wesley HURCH**, born 10 April 1938.

+ 225. m   iii.   **Robert Douglas HURCH**, born 19 November 1942.

+ 226. m   iv.   **Gilbert Leslie HURCH**, born 12 October 1944.

+ 227. m   v.   **Timothy Allen HURCH**, born 24 July 1948.

228. f   vi.   **Georgia Dawn HURCH**, born 23 April 1950. She married **Donald MERRIMAN** 17 October 1971. He was born 19 May 1948.

+ 229. f   vii.   **Avereil Janis HURCH**, born 4 March 1955.

230. f   viii.   **Billie Joy HURCH**, born 29 August 1956. She married **Harold PETERSON** 5 August 1973. He was born 6 October 1955.

151.   **Warren Frances[5] WEBSTER** (82.Daniel[4], 25.William[3], 4.Mary[2], 1.Jacob[1]) was born 20 March 1923 in Roxbury, Kansas. He is the son of Daniel Clay WEBSTER and Lillian KEEFER. He married **Margaret SPONGBERG** 24 January 1947. She was born 21 May 1926.

They had 5 children:

231. f   i.   **Sandra Sue WEBSTER**, born 17 March 1949. She married **Robert KELLY** 11 November 1970. He was born 9 March 1949.

+ 232. m   ii.   **Larry Wayne WEBSTER**, born 29 June 1951.

233. f   iii.   **Denise Ann WEBSTER**, born 12 March 1955. She married **Mark LYSELL** 16 February 1974. He was born 17 September 1950.

234. m   iv.   **Gary Dean WEBSTER**, born 16 March 1957, died 3 November 1974, at the age of 17.

235.   m   v.   **Jerry Lee WEBSTER**, born 1 October 1963.

- - - - - - - - - - -

152. Ronald Daniel⁵ WEBSTER (82.Daniel⁴, 25.William³, 4.Mary², 1.Jacob¹) was born 14 November 1925. He is the son of Daniel Clay WEBSTER and Lillian KEEFER. He married **Ruth FITE** 21 August 1946. She was born 6 September 1929.

They had 2 children:

+ 236. f   i.   **Katherine Ann WEBSTER**, born 14 September 1947.
237.   m   ii.   **Daniel Keith WEBSTER**, born 24 November 1953.

- - - - - - - - - - -

153. Alice Jane⁵ WEBSTER (82.Daniel⁴, 25.William³, 4.Mary², 1.Jacob¹) was born 4 February 1928. She is the daughter of Daniel Clay WEBSTER and Lillian KEEFER. She married **Darrell CARLSON** 1 May 1949. He was born 21 August 1921.

They had 2 children:

238. f   i.   **Alice Lorraine CARLSON**, born 19 November 1950. She married **Howard WEBB** 19 December 1972.
239.   m   ii.   **Curtiss Darrell CARLSON**, born 6 October 1954, died 21 December 1969, at the age of 15.

- - - - - - - - - -

154. Patricia Lillian⁵ WEBSTER (82.Daniel⁴, 25.William³, 4.Mary², 1.Jacob¹) was born 24 March 1931. She was the daughter of Daniel Clay WEBSTER and Lillian KEEFER. Patricia died 6 November 1979, at the age of 48. She married **Marvin JOHNSON** 26 December 1951. He was born 11 September 1931.

They had 3 children:

240. m   i.   **Paul Ryan JOHNSON**, born 29 September 1952.
241. f   ii. **Teresa Lynn JOHNSON**, born 22 May 1954, died in infancy 27 May 1954.
242. m   iii. **Greg Brian JOHNSON**, born 6 May 1955.

- - - - - - - - - -

157. Reginald Dale⁵ WEBSTER (85.Benjamin⁴, 25.William³, 4.Mary², 1.Jacob¹) was born 26 August 1911 in Canton, McPherson County, Kansas. He was the son of Benjamin Harrison WEBSTER and Laveta Fern OLDFIELD. Reginald died of a heart attack 2 July 1965 in Wichita, Sedgwick County, Kansas, at the age of 53. He married **Julia BERG** 2 October 1941 in Wichita, Sedgwick County, Kansas. She was born 14 October 1907 in Hillsboro, Marion County, Kansas. She was the daughter of Peter Paul BERG and Juliana SCHROEDER who were Dutch Mennonites. Julia died of a heart attack 13 March 1982 in Wichita,

Sedgwick County, Kansas, at the age of 74.[15]

> They had 2 children:

+ 243. m   i.   **Dale Douglas WEBSTER**, born 5 February 1945.

+ 244. m   ii.   **Larry Joe WEBSTER**, born 17 November 1946.

> Reginald had 1 stepchild:

+ 245. f   iii.   **Bonnie Lou CORNELSEN**, born 30 December 1930.

Julia also married (1) Herman David CORNELSEN 22 August 1929 in Newton, Reno County, Kansas; they divorced in 1932. He was born 8 February 1903 in Alne, Marion County, Kansas. Herman died 15 January 1952 in Wichita, Sedgwick County, Kansas, at the age of 48, and was buried 18 January 1952 in Peabody, Kansas.

Reginald started as an automobile mechanic in the garage at his father's dealership. He later was a tool and die maker for the Boeing Aircraft Company division in Wichita, Kansas for 20 years. During World War II, he helped build many B-17 and B-29 bombers. Later during the 1950s and 1960s, he was an inspector for B-47 and B-52 parts made in subcontractor facilities in Grand Prairie, Texas, and Hagerstown, Maryland. He also was a member of Albert Pike Masonic Lodge, Wichita Consistory and Midian Shrine. He was the author's father. He injured his leg in a shop

---

[15] Kansas birth certificate.

accident and limped most of his life. He was in poor health in middle age and died early.

- - - - - - - - - -

158.   Elaine   Maxine⁵   WEBSTER   (85.Benjamin⁴, 25.William³, 4.Mary², 1.Jacob¹) was born 24 February 1914 in Canton, McPherson County, Kansas. She is the daughter of Benjamin Harrison WEBSTER and Laveta Fern OLDFIELD. She married **Dore Verl WILSON** 6 November 1933 in Wichita, Sedgwick County, Kansas. He was born 10 December 1905 in Jay County, Indiana. He was the son of William Franklin WILSON and Jessie LEFEVER. Dore died 16 May 1966 in Guysville, Ohio, at the age of 60, and was buried 20 May 1966 in Parkersburg, Wood County, West Virginia.

They had 4 children:

+ 246. m   i.   **Rodney Dale WILSON**, born 27 October 1934.
+ 247. f   ii.   **Joan Dorothy WILSON**, born 19 October 1937.
+ 248. m   iii.   **Michael James WILSON**, born 15 March 1942.
+ 249. m   iv.   **Steven Ross WILSON**, born 28 July 1947.

Elaine kept many of the family records that appear in this genealogy. She has stayed in touch with most of the family members as they moved to all parts of the country.

- - - - - - - - - -

159. **Virginia Enola[5] WEBSTER** (85.Benjamin[4], 25.William[3], 4.Mary[2], 1.Jacob[1]) was born 6 August 1916 in McPherson, McPherson County, Kansas. She was the daughter of Benjamin Harrison WEBSTER and Laveta Fern OLDFIELD. Virginia died 5 July 1976 in Lyons, Rice County, Kansas, at the age of 59. She married **Noel Johnson KNIGHT** 16 July 1933 in Wellington, Kansas. He was born 1912 in McPherson, McPherson County, Kansas. Noel died in Kilgore, Texas.

They had 3 children:

+ 250. f   i.   **Shirley Enola KNIGHT**, born 5 July 1936.
251. m   ii.   **Donald KNIGHT**.
252. f   iii.   **Gloria KNIGHT**.

Virginia was a tall, blonde, beautiful woman. In middle age, she had many health problems that required several operations. After her death, her husband Noel, who was a successful oil service company owner, sold his business and moved to Texas where his son lived.

- - - - - - - - - -

161. **Randall Harry[5] WEBSTER** (85.Benjamin[4], 25.William[3], 4.Mary[2], 1.Jacob[1]) was born 31 March 1923 in Canton, McPherson County, Kansas. He was the son of Benjamin Harrison WEBSTER and Laveta Fern OLDFIELD. Randall died 15 June 1994 in Parkersburg, Wood County, West Virginia, at the age of 71. He married **Peggy HOUSER** 21 April 1942 in Wichita, Sedgwick County, Kansas. She was born 21 September 1924 in Wichita, Sedgwick County, Kansas. Peggy died 13 August 1973 in

New Orleans, Louisiana, at the age of 48.

They had 2 children:

+ 253. f   i.   **Pamela Kay WEBSTER,** born 21 November 1945.

+ 254. f   ii.   **Ginny Fern WEBSTER,** born 22 July 1947.

Randall went by Randy. He was a Marine during World War II. He was a car salesman for his father and continued in that work for most of his life. He and his family lived in Texas and Louisiana.

- - - - - - - - - - -

162. Bob Rex Alvin[5] WEBSTER (85.Benjamin[4], 25.William[3], 4.Mary[2], 1.Jacob[1]) was born 29 October 1925 in Canton, McPherson County, Kansas. He is the son of Benjamin Harrison WEBSTER and Laveta Fern OLDFIELD. He married **Ruth RIFFEL** 26 April 1946 in Newton, Kansas. She was born 29 March 1929 in Wichita, Sedgwick County, Kansas.

They had 1 child:

255. m   i.   **Bobby WEBSTER,** born about 1950 in Wichita, Kansas.

Bob was a Navy sailor in World War II and served in the Pacific. After the war, he and his family moved to Wichita, Kansas and then to Los Angeles, California. In the late 1970s, he bought Noel Knight's oil service business and returned to central Kansas. His wife Ruth owned and operated a restaurant in Lyons at the time. When the US oil business was in downturn in the mid-1980s, Bob and Ruth sold out and moved to Las Vegas to retire.

- - - - - - - - - - -

168. Elman J.[5] UNRUH (87.Bertha[4], 25.William[3], 4.Mary[2], 1.Jacob[1]) was born 31 January 1917 in Marion County, Kansas. He is the son of John F. UNRUH and Bertha Jane WEBSTER. He married (1) **Lvonne LINKE** September 1941; they divorced.

No children have yet been identified.

Elman married (2) **Melvia Layrie DILLON** 12 April 1947 in Las Vegas, Nevada.

They had 2 children:

+ 256. f   i.   **Barbara Elaine UNRUH**, born 12 June 1948.
257.   f   ii.   **Virginia Lee UNRUH**.

- - - - - - - - - - -

169. Clarice Elsie[5] UNRUH (87.Bertha[4], 25.William[3], 4.Mary[2], 1.Jacob[1]) was born 28 April 1918 in Marion County, Kansas. She is the daughter of John F. UNRUH and Bertha Jane WEBSTER. She married **Norman Ludwig HAEFNER** 23 December 1948 in Haven, Kansas.

They had 2 children:

+ 258. f   i.   **Sharon Lee HAEFNER**, born 8 February 1950.
259.   f   ii.   **Carol Lynne HAEFNER**, born 12 April 1954 in McPherson, Kansas. She married **Gary Lynn STUCKY** 17 March 1973.

- - - - - - - - - - -

170. Louis Daniel^5 UNRUH (87.Bertha^4, 25.William^3, 4.Mary^2, 1.Jacob^1) was born 24 July 1919 in Marion County, Kansas. He is the son of John F. UNRUH and Bertha Jane WEBSTER. He married (1) **Frankie HARPER**; they divorced.

No children have yet been identified.

Louis married (2) **Reatric MICK** December 1964.

They had 1 child:

260. m   i.   **Steve Louis UNRUH**, born 5 November 1965.

- - - - - - - - - - -

172. Erma Mae^5 UNRUH (87.Bertha^4, 25.William^3, 4.Mary^2, 1.Jacob^1) was born 12 September 1928 in Marion County, Kansas. She is the daughter of John F. UNRUH and Bertha Jane WEBSTER. She married **William C. HOLLEY** 16 March 1958 in Wichita, Kansas; they divorced.

They had 3 children:

261. f   i.   **Jennie Geneva HOLLEY**, born 9 May 1959 in Florida.

262. m   ii.   **Eugene Quentin HOLLEY**, born 26 April 1960 in McPherson, Kansas.

263. f   iii. **Ann Marie HOLLEY**, born 7 June 1963 in Lincoln, Nebraska.

- - - - - - - - - -
173. Doris Jane⁵ UNRUH (87.Bertha⁴, 25.William³, 4.Mary², 1.Jacob¹) was born 18 August 1932 in Marion County, Kansas. She is the daughter of John F. UNRUH and Bertha Jane WEBSTER. She married **Donald Lee FARMER** 22 June 1957 in McPherson, Kansas.

They had 5 children:

264. m i. **David Alan FARMER**, born 6 April 1958 in Wichita, Kansas.
265. f ii. **Denise Annette FARMER**, born 21 April 1961 in Wichita, Kansas.
266. f iii. **Debra Ann FARMER**, born 20 March 1962 in Colorado Springs, Colorada.
267. f iv. **Deidra Alane FARMER**, born 20 March 1962 in Colorado Springs, Colorada.
268. m v. **Daryl Lee FARMER**, born 18 February 1965 in Colorado Springs, Colorada.

- - - - - - - - - -
174. Jonas Boyd⁵ UNRUH (87.Bertha⁴, 25.William³, 4.Mary², 1.Jacob¹) was born 28 April 1934 in Hillsboro, Marion County, Kansas. He is the son of John F. UNRUH and Bertha Jane WEBSTER. He married **Francess Lorraine KLASSEN** 11 March 1962 in Inman, Kansas.

They had 1 child:

269. m i. **Brian J. UNRUH**, born 18 April 1963 in McPherson, Kansas.

- - - - - - - - - -

185. Howard Emerson[5] WEBSTER (102.Arthur[4], 30.Frehling[3], 4.Mary[2], 1.Jacob[1]) was born 20 November 1913 in Iowa County, Iowa. He was the son of Arthur H. WEBSTER and Blanche Bernice BUCK. Howard died 21 July 1991 in Iowa City, Iowa, at the age of 77. He married **Bernice Elizabeth DENNEY** 17 April 1948 in Ringgold County, Iowa. She was born 20 June 1919 in Ringgold County, Iowa.

They had 2 children:

270. f   i.   **Julia Christene WEBSTER**, born 12 November 1949 in Iowa City, Iowa. She married **Glenn THOMERSON** 1 June 1973 in Sarasota, Florida. He was born 19 October 1940 in Glasglow, Kentucky.

271. m   ii.   **David Denney WEBSTER**, born 9 October 1954 in Iowa City, Iowa. He married **Jill Charlene KING** 4 August 1996 in Ames, Iowa. She was born 1960.

CHAPTER 6

GENERATION NO. 6

The sixth generation of the descendants of Jacob and Mary Moomey is made up of their third great grandchildren. They lived primarily in the last half of the twentieth century and into the twenty first century. They participated in the Cold War and the Vietnam War. They are mostly city dwellers and are accustomed to high technology that their third great grandparents hardly could comprehend.

199. Donald Franklin[6] MOOMEY (119.Donald[5], 60.Clarence[4], 20.Henry[3], 3.John[2], 1.Jacob[1]) was born 3 April 1947 in Clarke County, Iowa. He is the son of Donald William MOOMEY and Leota Mae McBROOM. He married **Doris Florene ROBISON** 12 June 1977 in Osceola, Clarke County, Iowa. She was born 27 December 1954 in Leon, Iowa. She is the daughter of Billie D. ROBISON and Nadine WILLIAMS.

They had 2 children:
272. m   i.   **Ryan Scott MOOMEY**, born 25 June 1978 in Leon, Iowa.
273. f   ii.   **Amber Dawn MOOMEY**, born 11 April 1980 in Leon, Iowa.

- - - - - - - - - -

202. William Eugene[6] WEBSTER (122.Stanley[5], 72.William[4], 25.William[3], 4.Mary[2], 1.Jacob[1]) was born 28 February 1911 in Canton, McPherson County, Kansas. He was the son of Stanley Ross WEBSTER and Mabel A.

SPURRIER. William died 12 May 1969 in Barstow, San Bernardino County, California, at the age of 58. He married **Lelah Bernice NICHOLSON** 20 October 1931 in Lyons, Rice County, Kansas. She was born 18 September 1912 in Wellington, Sumner County, Kansas. Lelah died 10 April 1969 in Barstow, San Bernardino County, California, at the age of 56.

They had 2 children:

274. m   i.   **Richard Eugene WEBSTER**, born 10 December 1932 in Hutchinson, Harvey County, Kansas. He married **Doris MATTHEWS** 6 December 1952 in Glendale, Los Angeles County, California.

+ 275. f   ii.   **Carol Elaine WEBSTER**, born 25 January 1944.

- - - - - - - - - -

221. Barbara Kay[6] WEBSTER (149.Wendell[5], 82.Daniel[4], 25.William[3], 4.Mary[2], 1.Jacob[1]) was born 11 July 1944. She is the daughter of Wendell Sherwood WEBSTER and Dorothy KARLEY. She married **Ronald PORTER** 25 August 1966; they divorced.

They had 1 child:

276. m   i.   **Darin PORTER**, born 31 January 1967.

- - - - - - - - - -

223. Gerald Gene[6] HURCH (150.Wilma[5], 82.Daniel[4], 25.William[3], 4.Mary[2], 1.Jacob[1]) was born 16 August 1936.

He is the son of George HURCH and Wilma Allene WEBSTER. He married **Mary ANDERSON** September 1966. She was born 30 August 1942.

They had 1 child:

277. m   i.   **Monty   Wayne   HURCH,** born 25 December 1968.

- - - - - - - - - - -

224. Charles Wesley⁶ HURCH (150.Wilma⁵, 82.Daniel⁴, 25.William³, 4.Mary², 1.Jacob¹) was born 10 April 1938. He is the son of George HURCH and Wilma Allene WEBSTER. He married **Carolyn HALLOCK** 26 December 1965. She was born 26 November 1943.

They had 2 children:

278. f   i.   **Amanda   Jane   HURCH,** born 6 November 1971.
279. f   ii. **Erin   Elizabeth   HURCH,** born 28 February 1974.

- - - - - - - - - - -

225. Robert Douglas⁶ HURCH (150.Wilma⁵, 82.Daniel⁴, 25.William³, 4.Mary², 1.Jacob¹) was born 19 November 1942. He is the son of George HURCH and Wilma Allene WEBSTER. He married **Mildred GEORGE** 12 September 1964. She was born 5 February 1944.

They had 1 child:

280. m   i.   **David Lynn HURCH,** born 27 January 1965.

83

- - - - - - - - - -

226. Gilbert Leslie⁶ HURCH (150.Wilma⁵, 82.Daniel⁴, 25.William³, 4.Mary², 1.Jacob¹) was born 12 October 1944. He is the son of George HURCH and Wilma Allene WEBSTER. He married (1) **Sandra ALLEN** July 1965; they divorced.

They had 2 children:

281. m   i.   **Gilbert Allen HURCH**, born 30 March 1966.

282. f   ii.   **June Marie HURCH**, born 17 April 1967.

Gilbert married (2) **Judy SCHAAF** 12 May 1971. She was born 21 February 1950.

They had 1 child:

283. m   iii.   **Daniel Otis HURCH**, born 31 December 1973.

- - - - - - - - - -

227. Timothy Allen⁶ HURCH (150.Wilma⁵, 82.Daniel⁴, 25.William³, 4.Mary², 1.Jacob¹) was born 24 July 1948. He is the son of George HURCH and Wilma Allene WEBSTER. He married **Janet WALDSCHMIDT** 8 July 1967. She was born 31 May 1947.

They had 2 children:

284. m   i.   **Christopher John HURCH**, born 22 December 1971.

285. f   ii.   **Nicole Lynn HURCH**, born 1 November 1974.

- - - - - - - - - - -

229. Avereil Janis[6] **HURCH** (150.Wilma[5], 82.Daniel[4], 25.William[3], 4.Mary[2], 1.Jacob[1]) was born 4 March 1955. She is the daughter of George HURCH and Wilma Allene WEBSTER. She married **Charles BOYER** 8 December 1972. He was born 24 April 1953.

They had 1 child:

286. m i. **Richard Edward BOYER**, born 22 January 1974.

- - - - - - - - - - -

232. Larry Wayne[6] **WEBSTER** (151.Warren[5], 82.Daniel[4], 25.William[3], 4.Mary[2], 1.Jacob[1]) was born 29 June 1951. He is the son of Warren Frances WEBSTER and Margaret SPONGBERG. He married **Barbara SANDS** 12 January 1974. She was born 23 June 1955.

They had 1 child:

287. f i. **Tonya Maria WEBSTER**, born 25 September 1974.

- - - - - - - - - - -

236. Katherine Ann[6] **WEBSTER** (152.Ronald[5], 82.Daniel[4], 25.William[3], 4.Mary[2], 1.Jacob[1]) was born 14 September 1947. She is the daughter of Ronald Daniel WEBSTER and Ruth FITE. She married **William WELLBORN** 17 April 1970. He was born 12 August 1946.

They had 1 child:

288. f i. **Kathryn Jennifer WELLBORN**, born 5 August 1974.

85

- - - - - - - - - -

243. Dale Douglas[6] WEBSTER (157.Reginald[5], 85.Benjamin[4], 25.William[3], 4.Mary[2], 1.Jacob[1]) was born 5 February 1945 in Wichita, Kansas. He is the son of Reginald Dale WEBSTER and Julia BERG. He married **Kathleen Louise FERGUSON** 11 June 1966 in Wichita, Sedgwick County, Kansas. She was born 24 July 1944 in Wichita, Sedgwick County, Kansas. She is the daughter of Clifford Earl FERGUSON and Jean Ardis SOLTER.

They had 1 child:

+ 289. m   i.   **Douglas Clifford WEBSTER**, born 4 March 1969.

- - - - - - - - - -

244. Larry Joe[6] WEBSTER (157.Reginald[5], 85.Benjamin[4], 25.William[3], 4.Mary[2], 1.Jacob[1]) was born 17 November 1946 in Wichita, Sedgwick County, Kansas. He is the son of Reginald Dale WEBSTER and Julia BERG. He married **Sherry Jane OSBORN**.

They had 1 child:

290. f   i.   **Anita Marie LANDWEHR**.

- - - - - - - - - -

245. Bonnie Lou[6] CORNELSEN (stepchild of 157.Reginald[5], 85.Benjamin[4], 25.William[3], 4.Mary[2], 1.Jacob[1]) was born 30 December 1930 in Hillsboro, Marion County, Kansas. She is the daughter of Herman David CORNELSEN and Julia BERG. She married **William**

David CARROLL 8 October 1949 in Wichita, Sedgwick County, Kansas. He was born 8 December 1927 in Vinita, Craig County, Oklahoma. He is the son of Clem CARROLL and Nina Boyd BRYANT.

They had 4 children:

291. f   i.   **Sandra Lea CARROLL**, born 21 November 1951 in Wichita, Sedgwick County, Kansas. She married **David Charles SMITH** 12 November 1988 in Seattle, **Washington**. He was born 21 July 1953 in Seattle, Washington. He is the son of Benjamin Joseph SMITH and Barbara Jean **HOOVEN**. David is Executive **Vice** President of Seattle Financial Group.

+ 292. m   ii.   **David Alan CARROLL**, born 11 March 1954.

+ 293. f   iii.   **Teresa Diane CARROLL**, born 13 July 1960.

+ 294. f   iv.   **Debra Lynn CARROLL**, born 30 June 1966.

- - - - - - - - - -

246. Rodney Dale[6] WILSON (158.Elaine[5], 85.Benjamin[4], 25.William[3], 4.Mary[2], 1.Jacob[1]) was born 27 October 1934 in Hillsboro, Marion County, Kansas. He is the son of Dore Verl WILSON and Elaine Maxine WEBSTER. He married **Francis Joan GWYNN** 21 September 1953 in Parkersburg, Wood County, West Virginia. She was born 8 December

1935 in Parkersburg, Wood County, West Virginia. She is the daughter of William Frederick GWYNN and Ada Louella SNYDER.

They had 6 children:

+ 295. m   i.   **Steven Michael WILSON**, born 8 January 1954.

+ 296. f   ii.   **Deborah Sue WILSON**, born 14 September 1955.

+ 297. m   iii.   **Shawn Joseph WILSON, Sr.**, born 31 August 1957.

298. f   iv.   **Beth Ann WILSON**, born 6 November 1963 in Nowata, Oklahoma, died 17 August 1988 in Pawhuska, Osage County, Oklahoma, at the age of 24.

+ 299. m   v.   **David Patrick WILSON**, born 6 November 1965.

+ 300. m   vi.   **Phillip Timothy WILSON, Sr.**, born 4 October 1970.

- - - - - - - - - -

247. Joan Dorothy[6] WILSON (158.Elaine[5], 85.Benjamin[4], 25.William[3], 4.Mary[2], 1.Jacob[1]) was born 19 October 1937 in Odessa, Ector County, Texas. She is the daughter of Dore Verl WILSON and Elaine Maxine WEBSTER. She married **Marvin Arno PETTY** 10 June 1955 in Parkersburg, Wood County, West Virginia. He was born 15 March 1935 in Parkersburg, Wood County, West Virginia. He is the son of John Rex PETTY and Henrietta Murhl BAUMAN.

They had 5 children:

+ 301. f   i.   **Lucinda Jane PETTY**, born 28 December 1955.

+ 302. f   ii.   **Wanda Sue PETTY**, born 17 May 1957.

+ 303. f   iii.   **Cheryl Ann PETTY**, born 20 December 1958.

304. f   iv.   **Judith Lynn PETTY**, born 31 January 1960 in Parkersburg, Wood County, West Virginia.

305. f   v.   **Kelly Dianne PETTY**, born 14 May 1962 in Parkersburg, Wood County, West Virginia. She married **Berry John SMITH** in Parkersburg, Wood County, West Virginia; they divorced. He was born 30 May **1962** in Parkersburg, Wood County, West Virginia.

- - - - - - - - - -

248. Michael James[6] WILSON (158.Elaine[5], 85.Benjamin[4], 25.William[3], 4.Mary[2], 1.Jacob[1]) was born 15 March 1942 in Odessa, Ector County, Texas. He is the son of Dore Verl WILSON and Elaine Maxine WEBSTER. He married **Josephine Loraine SIMCIC** 29 December 1963 in Fairview County, West Virginia. She was born 13 November 1943 in Fairmont County, West Virginia.

They had 2 children:

+ 306. f   i.   **Cynthia Loraine WILSON**, born 29 March 1965.

+ 307. f   ii.   **Michele Lynette WILSON**, born 29 March 1965.

- - - - - - - - - - -

249. Steven Ross⁶ WILSON (158.Elaine⁵, 85.Benjamin⁴, 25.William³, 4.Mary², 1.Jacob¹) was born 28 July 1947 in Parkersburg, Wood County, West Virginia. He is the son of Dore Verl WILSON and Elaine Maxine WEBSTER. He married **Violet Louise LIOTTI** 3 June 1967 in Parkersburg, Wood County, West Virginia. She was born 26 May 1947 in Parkersburg, Wood County, West Virginia. She is the daughter of Charles LIOTTI and Mary MORELL.

They had 2 children:

+ 308. m   i.   **Anthony Michael WILSON**, born 16 January 1972.
+ 309. f   ii.   **Angela Renee WILSON**, born 4 December 1976.

- - - - - - - - - - -

250. Shirley Enola⁶ KNIGHT (159.Virginia⁵, 85.Benjamin⁴, 25.William³, 4.Mary², 1.Jacob¹) was born 5 July 1936 in Goessel, Kansas. She is the daughter of Noel Johnson KNIGHT and Virginia Enola WEBSTER. She married (1) **Gene PERSSON** 1962 in Los Angeles, California; they divorced.

They had 1 child:

310. f   i.   **Kaitlin PERSSON**, born 1 February 1964 in New York, New York.

Shirley married (2) **John Richard HOPKINS** 22 May 1970 in London, England. He was born 27 January 1931 in

London, England. John died 23 June 1998 in California, at
the age of 67.

They had 1 child:

311. f   ii.   **Sophie   Cybele   HOPKINS**,   born
                   26 November 1968 in New York,
                   New York.

Shirley Knight had recognizable acting talent in high school.
After graduation, she went to Hollywood, California to seek a
career in motion pictures. She successfully secured roles in
major movies in the 1960s, including "Sweet Bird of Youth"
and "Dark at the Top of the Stairs". She went on to act on the
Broadway stage and on television. She has had numerous
honors including the Tony Award, three Emmy Awards, two
Golden awards, two academy award nominations, the Venice
Film Festival Best Actress, the Jury prize at the Cannes Film
Festival (for producing the film "Dutchman"), the Joseph
Jefferson award, two Drama Desk nominations, Three
Golden Globe nominations, and nine Emmy nominations.
She holds an honorary Doctor of Fine Arts degree from Lake
Forrest College.

She has been politically active all her adult life and works for
Handgun Control Inc., the homeless, AIDS research, and
abused women. In the past she worked a great deal for civil
rights and for nuclear disarmament. For eighteen months she
toured the country with Eve Ensler's one woman play "The
Depot" directed by Joanne Woodward to help educate and
organize people to deal with the nuclear threat.

She is from Kansas and has helped to start a Festival in the town of Independence for William Inge. Each spring, she returns to honor a playwright. She has directed plays and has written and directed a musical film about the homeless. In 2000, she was named Kansan of the Year and was presented with a citation from the governor.

In her work as an actress, she is particularly proud of the following:

THEATRE:
THE THREE SISTERS directed by Lee Strasberg (Broadway)
LOSING TIME (written for her by John Hopkins) (Broadway)
LANDSCAPE OF THE BODY by John Guare (Drama Desk nomination, Joseph Jefferson award) (Chicago-Broadway)
A LOVELY SUNDAY FOR CREVE COEUR (written for her by Tennessee Williams) (Off-Broadway)
KENNEDY'S CHILDREN by Robert Patrick (Tony Award) (Broadway)
ECONOMIC NECESSITY (written for her by John Hopkins) (England)
ABSENT FOREVER (written for her by John Hopkins) (Cleveland-PBS)
THE CHERRY ORCHARD (directed by Lucien Pintilie)(Arena Stage)
THE GLASS MENAGERIE (directed by Emily Mann) (McCarter)
THE YOUNG MAN FROM ATLANTA (written by Horton Foote, Tony award nomination)

CINEMA:
THE DARK AT THE TOP OF THE STAIRS (directed by Delbert Mann, Academy Award nomination, Golden Globe award)
SWEET BIRD OF YOUTH (directed by Richard Brooks, Academy Award nomination, Golden Globe nomination) PETULIA (directed by Richard Lester)
DUTCHMAN (Best Actress Venice, Critics prize Cannes, directed by Anthony Harvey)
THE GROUP (directed by Sidney Lumet)

THE RAIN PEOPLE (written for her and directed by Francis Ford Coppola)
ENDLESS LOVE (directed by Franco Zefferelli)
STUART SMALLEY (directed by Harold Ramis)
AS GOOD AS IT GETS (directed by James Brooks)
THE DEVINE SECRETS OF THE YA-YA SISTERHOOD

TELEVISION:
MISS JULIE by August Strindberg (CBC) THE COUNTRY GIRL by Clifford Odets (NBC)
THE LIE by Ingmar Bergman (CBS)
Three plays for British Television written for her by John Hopkins.
PLAYING FOR TIME by Arthur Miller (Emmy nomination) THIRTY SOMETHING (Emmy Award, Two Emmy nominations, directed by Edward Zwick)
LAW AND ORDER (Emmy nomination)
THE McMARTIN TRIAL (Emmy award, Golden Globe award)
MAGGIE WINTERS (TV SERIES)

Miss Knight was married to the writer John Hopkins, until his death in 1998. She has two daughters, Kaitlin Hopkins and Sophie Hopkins. John Hopkins adopted Kaitlin, and she took his surname. Kaitlin is an actress, and Sophie is a writer. Shirley also has a stepdaughter, Dr. Justine Hopkins. Justine teaches in London and has just published a biography about her step-grandfather, the sculptor and painter, Michael Ayrton.

Shirley's first husband was actor and theatrical producer Gene Persson, who first appeared as a child actor in the Ma and Pa Kettle series of movies in the 1950s.

Figure 9 – Shirley Knight
MGM Portrait from Early 1960s

Shirley's second husband, John Hopkins, was a well-known playwright. He began writing for television in the early sixties in England. A selection of the work he produced includes:

Original television plays:
"Break-up" - Granada TV - 1958
"A Woman Comes Home" - BBC - 1961
"A Chance of Thunder" - (six-part thriller serial) - BBC - 1961
"Z Cars" - (police series - 54 episodes) - BBC - 1962/1964 "Walk a Tight Circle" - BBC - 1962
"I Took My Little World Away" - ATV - 1963
"Horror of Darkness" - BBC - 1963
"Some Place of Safety" - (an opera for television) - BBC - 1964
"A Man Like Orpheus" - (a ballet for television) - BBC - 1964
"Fable" - BBC - 1964
"A Game - like - Only a Game" - BBC - 1965
"Talking to a Stranger" - (four plays for television) - BBC - 1965
"Beyond the Sunrise" - BBC - 1967
"Walk into the Dark" - BBC - 1971
"Some Distant Shadow" - Granada TV - 1971
"That Quiet Earth"- BBC - 1971
"Fathers and Families" - (six plays for television) - BBC - 1976
"A Story to Frighten the Children" - BBC - 1978
"Hiroshima" - ShowTime Cable TV - 1995

Adaptations:
"The Small Back Room" - (play for television from the novel written by Nigel Balchin) - BBC - 1958
"Mine Own Executioner" - (play for television from the novel written by Nigel Balchin) - BBC - 1959
"Dancers in Mourning" - (six-part mystery serial from the novel written by Margery Allingham) - BBC - 1959
"Death of a Ghost" - (six-part mystery serial from the novel written by Margery Allingham) - BBC - 1960
"Parade, End" - (three plays for television from the novels written by

Ford Madox Ford) - BBC - 1964

"The Gambler" - (two-part serial from the novel written by Feodor Dostoevsky) - BBC -1963

"Smiley, People" - (six-part serial from the novel written by John Le Carre) - BBC - 1984

"Codename Kyril" - (four hour mini series for television from the novel written by John Trenhaile) - Thames Television - 1987

Films:

"Two Left Feet " - British Lion - (shared credit) - 1963 "Thunderball" - United Artists - (shared credit) - 1965 "Virgin Soldiers" - British Lion - (shared credit) - 1967

"The Offence" - United Artists - 1972

"Murder by Decree" - Avco Embassy - 1978

"The Holcroft Covenant" - Universal - (shared credit) - 1985

Plays:

"This Story of Yours" - London - (premiere) - Royal Court Theatre - 1968 Stuttgart - 1969 New Haven - 1982 Hampstead Theatre Club - 1987 Buenos Aires - 1995

"Find Your Way Home" - London - (premiere) - Open Space - 1970 New York - (Brooks Atkinson) - 1973 Frankfurt - (Kleist Theatre) - 1995

"Economic Necessity" - Leicester - (premiere) - (Haymarket) - 1973

"Next of Kin" - London - (premiere) - (National Theatre) - 1974

"Valedictorian" - (premiere) - Williston Northampton School - 1978

"Losing Time" - New York - (premiere) - (Manhattan Theatre Club) - 1979 Hamburg - (Berlin and Vienna) - 1983

"Absent Forever" - (premiere) - Great Lakes Theatre Festival - 1987

Born in London, John Hopkins spent his early years in Wimbledon. After National Service, he went up to St Catharine, College, Cambridge to read English. After graduation he joined the BBC as a studio manager, and subsequently, as a Producer. He left the BBC and went to Granada Television for two years, where he began to write; at first for television, subsequently for the cinema, and eventually, for the theatre.

He continued to work in all three dramatic media; most recently, for the theatre, "Without Father, Without Son" and "The Mary Plays" for the cinema, "The Cleaning Lady" and "Sing Your Own Song", and for television, "Hiroshima".

Hopkins won the British Screen Writer, Guild Award for his work on dramatic series two years in succession for "Z Cars" in 1962 and 1963; the British Director, Guild Award for his mini-series "Talking to a Stranger" in 1966; and in 1969, for his contribution to "Masterpiece Theatre", an Emmy Award. He was nominated for an Edgar Allan Poe Award for his screenplay "Murder by Decree" in 1978; and nominated for a Cable Ace Award in 1995 for his television movie "Hiroshima" on ShowTime Cable Television. He won the HUMANITAS PRIZE for "Hiroshima". Mr. Hopkins is one of only two writers listed in the Encyclopedia Britannica for his contribution to television.

- - - - - - - - - -

253. Pamela Kay[6] WEBSTER (161.Randall[5], 85.Benjamin[4], 25.William[3], 4.Mary[2], 1.Jacob[1]) was born 21 November 1945 in Lyons, Kansas. She is the daughter of Randall Harry WEBSTER and Peggy HOUSER. She married **Leo Quinton NASH, Jr.** 7 March 1969 in New Orleans, Louisiana. He was born 12 February 1940 in New Orleans, Louisiana. Leo, Jr. died 19 April 1998 in Slidel, Louisiana, at the age of 58.

They had 2 children:

312. f   i.   **Stacey Ann NASH**, born 2 October 1969 in New Orleans, Louisiana. She

married **Barry Gene BRACK, Jr.** 17 February 1995. He was born 14 November 1970 in Millington, Tennessee.

+ 313. m   ii.   **Leo Quinton NASH, III**, born 29 July 1974.

- - - - - - - - - -

254. Ginny Fern⁶ WEBSTER (161.Randall⁵, 85.Benjamin⁴, 25.William³, 4.Mary², 1.Jacob¹) was born 22 July 1947 in Amarillo, Texas.   She is the daughter of Randall Harry WEBSTER and Peggy HOUSER.   She married (1) **Joseph Jules BLANCHARD, Sr.** 18 June 1966 in New Orleans, Louisiana.   He was born 28 August 1946 in New Orleans, Louisiana. Joseph, Sr. died 29 July 2001 in New Orleans, Louisiana, at the age of 54.

They had 2 children:

+ 314. m   i.   **Joseph Jules BLANCHARD, Jr.**, born 5 July 1967.
315. f   ii.   **Peggy BLANCHARD**, born 15 October 1975 in Metairie, Louisiana

Ginny married (2) **Robert Joseph BONNETTE** 29 September 2001 in New Orleans, Louisiana. He was born 6 February 1962 in New Orleans, Louisiana.

No children have yet been identified.

- - - - - - - - - - -

256. Barbara Elaine[6] UNRUH (168.Elman[5], 87.Bertha[4], 25.William[3], 4.Mary[2], 1.Jacob[1]) was born 12 June 1948. She is the daughter of Elman J. UNRUH and Melvia Layrie DILLON. She married (1) **Timothy McEVERS** 1966; they divorced.

They had 1 child:

316. f   i.   **Melanie Shanna McEVERS**, born **20 October** 1967.

Barbara married (2) **Lawrence NEWMAN** 11 July 1971.

They had 2 children:

317. m   ii.   **Keith Andrew NEWMAN**, born 7 June 1972.
318. f   iii.   **Wendy Collete NEWMAN**, born 28 February 1974.

- - - - - - - - - - -

258. Sharon Lee[6] HAEFNER (169.Clarice[5], 87.Bertha[4], 25.William[3], 4.Mary[2], 1.Jacob[1]) was born 8 February 1950 in Herington, Kansas. She is the daughter of Norman Ludwig HAEFNER and Clarice Elsie UNRUH. She married **Steven Lowell BLAZER** 29 November 1968.

They had 1 child:

319. f   i.   **Stacey Lynne BLAZER**, born 12 March 1970.

CHAPTER 7

GENERATION NO. 7

The people of the seventh generation are the fourth great grandchildren of Jacob and Mary Moomey. They are living in the computer age and are continuing to expand the family into the future.

275. Carol Elaine[7] **WEBSTER** (202.William[6], 122.Stanley[5], 72.William[4], 25.William[3], 4.Mary[2], 1.Jacob[1]) was born 25 January 1944 in Los Angeles, Los Angeles County, California. She is the daughter of William Eugene WEBSTER and Lelah Bernice NICHOLSON. She married **Larry Morris MOONEY** 29 September 1962 in Barstow, San Bernardino County, California; they divorced. He was born 9 February 1942 in Charlotte, Mecklebery County, North Carolina. He is the son of Lee Morris MOONEY and Frances Isabelle WILSON.

They had 3 children:

m   i.   **William Lee MOONEY**, born 10 November 1963.

f   ii.   **Christine Elaine MOONEY**, born 17 August 1966.

m   iii.   **Timothy Andrew MOONEY**, born 16 November 1969.

- - - - - - - - - -

289. Douglas Clifford[7] **WEBSTER** (243.Dale[6], 157.Reginald[5], 85.Benjamin[4], 25.William[3], 4.Mary[2], 1.Jacob[1]) was born 4 March 1969 in Carswell AFB, Fort

Worth, Tarrant County, Texas. He is the son of Dale Douglas WEBSTER and Kathleen Louise FERGUSON. He married (1) **Evelyn Marie ZOHLEN** 22 April 1995 in San Antonio, Texas; they divorced. She was born 25 August 1966 in Dallas, Dallas County, Texas. She is the daughter of Paul James ZOHLEN and Patricia Ann HARRISON.

They had no children.

Douglas married (2) **Anne Marie PRIESTAP** 17 June 2000 in Austin, Texas. She was born 23 August 1973 in Warren, Ohio. She is the daughter of Terry Edward PRIESTAP and Joan Theresa PANE.

They had 1 child:

m   i.   **Ian Havre WEBSTER**, born 10 February 2002.

Anne also married (1) John Mark MATKIN 1995; they divorced.

Douglas has 1 stepchild:

m   i.   **William Cole MATKIN**, born 11 Apr 1997 in San Antonio, Texas. He is the biological son of John Mark **MATKIN** and Anne Marie **PRIESTAP**.

- - - - - - - - - -

292. David Alan[7] CARROLL (245.Bonnie[6], stepchild of 157.Reginald[5], 85.Benjamin[4], 25.William[3], 4.Mary[2], 1.Jacob[1]) was born 11 March 1954 in Wichita, Sedgwick

County, Kansas. He is the son of William David CARROLL and Bonnie Lou CORNELSEN. He married (1) **Pamela Jean CARNER** 24 September 1976 in Kirkland, Washington; they divorced 6 Sep 1985. She was born 17 March 1954 in San Diego, California. She was the daughter of Duane E. CARNER and Charlene T. [————?————] . Pamela died of cancer 6 April 2002 in Federal Way, Washington, at the age of 48.

They had 1 child:

m i. **David Alan CARROLL, Jr.,** born 16 February 1984.

David married (2) **Mary Catherine SHIGLEY** 13 July 1986 in Kirkland, Washington; they divorced 26 Jan 1993. She was born 17 November 1958 in Seattle, Washington. She is the daughter of Walter Raymond Francis Michael SHIGLEY and Ruth Marie [————?————] .

They had 1 child:

m ii. **Mathew Raymond CARROLL,** born 15 May 1989.

- - - - - - - - - -

293. Teresa Diane[7] **CARROLL** (245.Bonnie[6], stepchild of 157.Reginald[5], 85.Benjamin[4], 25.William[3], 4.Mary[2], 1.Jacob[1]) was born 13 July 1960 in Wichita, Sedgwick County, Kansas. She is the daughter of William David CARROLL and Bonnie Lou CORNELSEN. She married **Howard Leroi MURRAY** 3 May 1986 in Mercer Island, Washington. He was born 8 June 1962 in Alton, Illinois. He is the son of Kevin FRYE and Priscilla Elaine MURRAY.

They had 2 children:

f   i.   **Tiana Nicole MURRAY**, born 8 June 1988.

m   ii.   **Jorel Cameron MURRAY**, born 1 August 1992.

- - - - - - - - - -

294. Debra Lynn[7] CARROLL (245.Bonnie[6], stepchild of 157.Reginald[5], 85.Benjamin[4], 25.William[3], 4.Mary[2], 1.Jacob[1]) was born 30 June 1966 in Bellevue, King County, Washington. She is the daughter of William David CARROLL and Bonnie Lou CORNELSEN. Her spouse has not been identified.

They had 1 child:

f   i.   **Natasha Lenai CARROLL**, born 25 March 1992.

- - - - - - - - - -

295. Steven Michael[7] WILSON (246.Rodney[6], 158.Elaine[5], 85.Benjamin[4], 25.William[3], 4.Mary[2], 1.Jacob[1]) was born 8 January 1954 in Parkersburg, Wood County, West Virginia. He is the son of Rodney Dale WILSON and Francis Joan GWYNN. He married **Ruth ENG** 11 August 1979 in Pawhuska, Osage County, Oklahoma. She was born 24 May 1953 in Chicago, Illinois. She is the daughter of Fred ENG and Doreen HUI.

They had 2 children:

m   i.   **Joshua Michael WILSON**, born

15 November 1980.

f   ii.   **Michelle Nicole WILSON**, born 4 February 1984.

- - - - - - - - - - -

296. Deborah Sue[7] WILSON (246.Rodney[6], 158.Elaine[5], 85.Benjamin[4], 25.William[3], 4.Mary[2], 1.Jacob[1]) was born 14 September 1955 in Parkersburg, Wood County, West Virginia. She is the daughter of Rodney Dale WILSON and Francis Joan GWYNN. She married **Laban Marchmont MILES, II** 2 March 1973 in Miami, Ottawa County, Oklahoma. He was born 20 November 1953 in Pawhuska, Osage County, Oklahoma. He is the son of Laban Marchmont MILES, I and Annetta LABADIE.

They had 2 children:

f   i.   **Angelia Dawn MILES**, born 18 July 1973.

m   ii.   **Laban Marchmont MILES, III**, born 1 November 1977.

- - - - - - - - - - -

297. Shawn Joseph[7] WILSON, Sr. (246.Rodney[6], 158.Elaine[5], 85.Benjamin[4], 25.William[3], 4.Mary[2], 1.Jacob[1]) was born 31 August 1957 in Parkersburg, Wood County, West Virginia. He is the son of Rodney Dale WILSON and Francis Joan GWYNN. He married **Ruby Elaine WINKLER** 8 August 1980 in Joplin, Missouri. She was born 6 March 1958 in Denver, Colorado. She is the daughter of Donald Howard WINKLER and Ruby Eleanor MEADE.

105

They had 3 children:

m   i.   **Shawn Joseph WILSON, Jr.,** born 1 March 1981.

f   ii.   **Tiffani Gwynn WILSON,** born 7 February 1983.

m   iii.   **Koty Ditto WILSON,** born 17 September 1996.

- - - - - - - - - -

299. David Patrick[7] WILSON (246.Rodney[6], 158.Elaine[5], 85.Benjamin[4], 25.William[3], 4.Mary[2], 1.Jacob[1]) was born 6 November 1965 in Nowata, Oklahoma. He is the son of Rodney Dale WILSON and Francis Joan GWYNN. He married (1) **Melanie QUINTON.** She was the daughter of Joe QUINTON and Sharon [————?————] . She is an Osage-Seneca Indian.

They had 1 child:

f   i.   **Haylee Elizabeth WILSON,** born 16 September 1994.

David married (2) **Ramona Danielle SCOTT** 20 February 1999 in Eureka Springs, Arkansas. She was born Osage Indian 29 May 1970 in Pawhuska, Osage County, Oklahoma. She is the daughter of Carol BAYHYL.

No children have yet been identified.

- - - - - - - - - -

300. Phillip Timothy[7] WILSON, Sr. (246.Rodney[6], 158.Elaine[5], 85.Benjamin[4], 25.William[3], 4.Mary[2], 1.Jacob[1]) was born 4 October 1970 in Pawhuska, Osage County, Oklahoma. He is the son of Rodney Dale WILSON and Francis Joan GWYNN. He married (1) **Brenda SMITH** 25 August 1988 in Pawhuska, Osage County, Oklahoma. She was born Seneca Indian 26 October 1969. She is the daughter of Don SMITH and Nancy FORTNY.

They had 2 children:

m   i.   **Phillip Timothy WILSON, Jr.**, born 24 January 1989.

f   ii.   **Kamree Danielle WILSON**, born 11 November 1992.

Phillip, Sr. married (2) **Brandi Jean SPENCER** 23 April 1999 in Catossa, Oklahoma. She was born Chocotaw Indian 1 November 1976 in Tulsa, Oklahoma. She is the daughter of Edward SPENCER and Wanda Jean JONES.

They had 3 children:

m   iii.   **Patrick Spencer WILSON**, born 28 January 1997.

m   iv.   **Tyler Christian WILSON**, born 13 May 1998.

m   v.   **Derek Ryan WILSON**, born 1 December 2001.

- - - - - - - - - -

301. Lucinda Jane[7] PETTY (247.Joan[6], 158.Elaine[5], 85.Benjamin[4], 25.William[3], 4.Mary[2], 1.Jacob[1]) was born 28 December 1955 in Parkersburg, Wood County, West Virginia. She is the daughter of Marvin Arno PETTY and

Joan Dorothy WILSON. She married **David Robert SNIDER** 31 August 1974 in Parkersburg, Wood County, West Virginia. He was born 26 February 1954 in Toledo, Lucas County, Ohio. He is the son of Edward Wetzel SNIDER and Martha Jean MULLINEX.

They had 2 children:

m   i.   **Jason David SNIDER**, born 17 January 1977.

f   ii.   **Christa Diane SNIDER**, born 8 June 1979.

- - - - - - - - - -

302. Wanda Sue[7] PETTY (247.Joan[6], 158.Elaine[5], 85.Benjamin[4], 25.William[3], 4.Mary[2], 1.Jacob[1]) was born 17 May 1957 in Parkersburg, Wood County, West Virginia. She is the daughter of Marvin Arno PETTY and Joan Dorothy WILSON. She married (1) **Karl Wayne KIRBY** 1976 in Parkersburg, Wood County, West Virginia; they divorced. He was born 12 October 1952 in Jacksonville, Florida. He is the son of Junior Karl KIRBY and Doris Jean McKIBBEN.

They had 2 children:

f   i.   **Michelle Renee KIRBY**, born 26 August 1976.

f   ii.   **Rebecca Diane KIRBY**, born 19 January 1978.

Wanda married (2) **James Andrew MACE, Sr.**.

They had 2 children:

m   iii.   **James Andrew MACE, Jr.,** born 29 September 1992.

m   iv.   **Tyler Levi MACE,** born 26 October 1993.

- - - - - - - - - - -

303. Cheryl Ann[7] PETTY (247.Joan[6], 158.Elaine[5], 85.Benjamin[4], 25.William[3], 4.Mary[2], 1.Jacob[1]) was born 20 December 1958 in Parkersburg, Wood County, West Virginia. She is the daughter of Marvin Arno PETTY and Joan Dorothy WILSON. She married **James Raymond ULLOM** 25 June 1983 in Waverly, Wood County, West Virginia. He was born 21 September 1958 in Salem, Columbiana County, Ohio. He is the son of Cecil Otto ULLOM and Marjorie Ann DRISCOLL.

They had 3 children:

m   i.   **Christopher Daniel ULLOM,** born 25 April 1985, died 12 April 2002.

m   ii.   **Nathanial Ryan ULLOM,** born 18 June 1987.

m   iii.   **Brandon James ULLOM,** born 15 December 1988.

- - - - - - - - - - -

306. Cynthia Loraine[7] WILSON (248.Michael[6], 158.Elaine[5], 85.Benjamin[4], 25.William[3], 4.Mary[2], 1.Jacob[1]) was born 29 March 1965 in Amarillo, Texas. She is the daughter of Michael James WILSON and Josephine Loraine SIMCIC. She married _____ **HUCKABEE.**

They had 1 child:

f   i.   **Diana L. WILSON**, born 22 September 1983.

- - - - - - - - - -

307. Michele Lynette[7] WILSON (248.Michael[6], 158.Elaine[5], 85.Benjamin[4], 25.William[3], 4.Mary[2], 1.Jacob[1]) was born 29 March 1965 in Amarillo, Texas. She is the daughter of Michael James WILSON and Josephine Loraine SIMCIC. She married _____ **WINSTEAD.**

They had 3 children:

m   i.   **Michael Joseph Verl WILSON**, born 29 January 1983.

m   ii.   **Christopher D. PATLAN**, born 3 November 1984.

m   iii.   **Aaron D. PATLAN**, born 12 March 1986.

- - - - - - - - - -

308. Anthony Michael[7] WILSON (249.Steven[6], 158.Elaine[5], 85.Benjamin[4], 25.William[3], 4.Mary[2], 1.Jacob[1]) was born 16 January 1972 in Parkersburg, Wood County, West Virginia. He is the son of Steven Ross WILSON and Violet Louise LIOTTI. He married **Cathleen Myer McCARTHY** 21 August 1999 in Parkersburg, Wood County, West Virginia. She was the daughter of John McCARTHY and Marlene [———?———] .

They had 1 child:

m   i.   **Dylan Michael WILSON**, born 11 December 1999.

- - - - - - - - - -

309. Angela Renee[7] WILSON (249.Steven[6], 158.Elaine[5], 85.Benjamin[4], 25.William[3], 4.Mary[2], 1.Jacob[1]) was born 4 December 1976 in Parkersburg, Wood County, West Virginia. She is the daughter of Steven Ross WILSON and Violet Louise LIOTTI. She married **Luca Dru KNAPP** 25 September 1999 in Parkersburg, Wood County, West Virginia. He was born 16 May 1977 in Parkersburg, Wood County, West Virginia. Luca died 26 September 2001 in Louisville, Jefferson County, Kentucky, at the age of 24, and was buried in Parkersburg, Wood County, West Virginia.

They had 1 child:

 f i. **Sydney Renee KNAPP**, born 15 August 2001.

- - - - - - - - - -

313. Leo Quinton[7] NASH, III (253.Pamela[6], 161.Randall[5], 85.Benjamin[4], 25.William[3], 4.Mary[2], 1.Jacob[1]) was born 29 July 1974 in New Orleans, Louisiana. He is the son of Leo Quinton NASH, Jr. and Pamela Kay WEBSTER. He married **Angie Lorraine MARKS** 14 February 1996; they divorced.

They had 1 child:

 f i. **Katie Meshail NASH**, born 10 September 1995.

- - - - - - - - - -

314. Joseph Jules[7] BLANCHARD, Jr. (254.Ginny[6],

111

161.Randall^5, 85.Benjamin^4, 25.William^3, 4.Mary^2, 1.Jacob^1) was born 5 July 1967 in New Orleans, Louisiana. He is the son of Joseph Jules BLANCHARD, Sr. and Ginny Fern WEBSTER. He married **Tammy Darlene COLLINS** 23 July 1987 in New Orleans, Louisiana. She was born 12 July 1963 in New Orleans, Louisiana.

They had 2 children:

m   i.   **Justin Joseph BLANCHARD**, born 14 September 1987.

f   ii.   **Maegan Rae BLANCHARD**, born 3 February 1992

INDEX OF NAMES

Laban Marchmont, I, 105
Laban Marchmont, II
  [1953-], 105
Laban Marchmont, III
  [1977-], 105
MILLER
  _____, 65
  Lota, 65
  Martha Gay [1872-
    1899], 23
  William I, 23
MISSENGER
  Lavera, 24
MOOMEY
  Amber Dawn [1980-],
    81
  Ambert, 26
  Betsy [1826-1880], 3, 18
  Bruce [1876-1951], 26,
    46
  Carl Henry [1894-1978],
    44
  Caroline, 10
  Carrie [-1911], 25
  Catherine [1831-], 3, 20,
    39
  Christian [1835-], 3
  Christina [1812-1894],
    2, 9, 23
  Clarence Mitchell
    [1873-1950], 25, 43, 63
  Clarinda C. [1849-

1927], 25, 43
Cora [1858-1935], 26, 47
Cordelia [1844-], 18
Cullen [1886-1978], 26
Donald Franklin [1947-
  ], 63, 81
Donald William [1915-
  ], 46, 63, 81
Doris Florene [1954-],
  81
Echo Lewis [1905-
  1907], 45
Edith [1897-1923], 44
Effa (--) [1827-], 18
Eithel Pauline [1902-],
  45
Eletty B., 20
Elizabeth (--) [1817-],
  10, 24, 25
Ella M., 19
Frank H. [1868-1946],
  25
Freeling Sylvester
  [1875-1932], 19
Gerald Burr [1897-
  1968], 44
Grace Marlee [1892-
  1945], 43
Harriet Roseta, 19
Harry Bryan [1899-
  1921], 44
Hazel Irene [1910-

127

Enos, 65
Ethel May [1884-1932], 39
Evelyn, 56
Evelyn Marie (Zohlen) [1966-], 102
Everett Winston [1914-], 51, 67
Florence [1871-], 29
Florence Rowena (Anderson) [1855-], 39, 59
Forrest, 65
Francis Ellen [1863-1951], 37
Frehling Sylvester [1851-1929], 12, 39, 59
Gary Dean [1957-1974], 69
Gerald [1907-1990], 50, 65
Geraldine, 64
Geraldine Marilyn [1918-1964], 64
Gertrude, 48
Ginny Fern [1947-], 75, 98, 112
Gloria, 65
Gretel [-1967], 67
Harriet [1838-1916], 11, 27
Howard, 47
Howard Emerson

[1913-1991], 59, 79
Howard Lincoln [1881-1969], 30, 49, 65, 66, 67
Ian Havre [2002-], 102
Inez Ruth [1918-], 53
Jacob [1847-1847], 12
James [1916-1997], 64
Jennie Mae, 38
Jennie Orilla [1871-1872], 38
Jerry Lee [1963-], 70
Jill Charlene [1960-], 79
John Charles [1856-1925], 12
John Ellsworth [1869-1941], 29, 48
John H. [1814-1876], 11, 26, 27, 28, 37, 38, 39
John Raymond, 48
Joseph Norman [1865-], 27
Josephine Maude [1880-aft 1972], 38
Julia (Berg) [1907-1982], 71, 86
Julia Christene [1949-], 79
June (Fuller), 65
Katherine Ann [1947-], 70, 85
Kathleen Louise (Ferguson) [1944-],

Peter, 9
Susan Ann [1851-], 9,
  23
YOAKAM
  Eliza Hannah [1839-
    1921], 26
  Ella, 19
  Joseph [1817-], 27
  Nancy, 27
YODER
  Daniel E., 39
  Elmer E., 38
  Ethel May [1884-1932],
    39
  Josephine Maude [1880-
    aft 1972], 38
ZEPP
  Lloyd B., 46
  Nellie Arline [1912-
    1984], 46
ZOHLEN
  Evelyn Marie [1966-],
    102
  Patricia Ann (Harrison)
    [1945-], 102
  Paul James [1943-], 102

About the Author

Dale Douglas Webster is the son of Reginald and Julia (Berg) Webster. He was born on February 5, 1945 in Wichita, Kansas. Dale graduated from Wichita State University in 1967 with a Bachelor of Arts degree in mathematics and from the University of Oregon in 1976 with a Master of Business Administration degree.

He served over twenty years within the U.S. and overseas as an Air Force officer in meteorology, transportation, and computer science. After retiring from the U.S. Air Force in 1987, Dale has worked in the Washington, DC metropolitan area as a computer software consultant.

Dale has been married to Kathleen Ferguson for thirty six years. She is the daughter of Clifford Earl and Jean Ardis

(Solter) Ferguson. Kathleen and Dale have one son, Douglas. Doug and his wife, Anne, have two sons, Cole and Ian.

He has been researching his family history for fourteen years. He is a member of the Mayflower Society, the Alden Kindred, and the Sons of the American Revolution. If you have any information that can update or expand this work, please contact:

Dale_Webster@yahoo.com

www.ingramcontent.com/pod-product-compliance
Lightning Source LLC
Chambersburg PA
CBHW072152270326
41930CB00011B/2400